BIRDS
COPING WITH
AN OBSESSION

BIRDS
COPING WITH
AN OBSESSION

DEREK MOORE

One man's journey through 70 years of birdwatching

NEW
HOLLAND

First published in 2013 by New Holland Publishers
London • Cape Town • Sydney • Auckland
www.newhollandpublishers.com

Garfield House, 86–88 Edgware Road, London W2 2EA, UK
Wembley Square, First Floor, Solan Road, Cape Town, 8001, South Africa
Unit 1, 66 Gibbes Street, Chatswood, NSW 2067, Australia
218 Lake Road, Northcote, Auckland, New Zealand

A CIP catalogue record for this book is available from the British Library.

ISBN 978 1 84773 952 0

Publisher and editor: Simon Papps
Designer: Keisha Galbraith
Production: Olga Dementiev

Printed and bound in China by Toppan Leefung Printing Ltd

Keep up with New Holland Publishers on Facebook
http://www.facebook.com/NewHollandPublishers

All photographs by Derek Moore, except for the following: Steve Aylward
(pages 101, 111, 121, 130 and 137), Tim Brown (50), *East Anglian Daily
Times* (84), Leslie Freeman (37), David Hosking (131, 174 and 189), Eric
Hosking (54), Beryl Moore (141 and 211), Xavier Muñoz-Contreras (back
flap of jacket), Martin Nugent (71), Wayne Simpson (255), Barry Stewart
(235), Roger Tidman (75), David Tomlinson (82), Jan Tomlinson (81)
and Markus Varesvuo (jacket).

Contents

Forewords by Bill Oddie and Chris Packham   7

1. FROM THE WOMB   13
2. AFTER FLEDGING   33
3. PAIRING UP   49
4. BREEDING SUCCESS   64
5. CONSERVATION BECKONS   90
6. TRAVELLING FOR BIRDS   155
7. RETIREMENT OF A SORT   224
8. WHAT OF THE FUTURE   245

Other Natural History Books by New Holland   266

Dedication

This book is dedicated to my wonderful wife Beryl, my daughter Bronwen, my son Jeremy and his wife Saskia and their children Morris, Tara and Holly.

All have indulged my obsession and all at times have joined in.

Foreword

by Bill Oddie

"And then I hit him!" To me that is Derek's catchphrase.
I have never actually heard him say it – let alone do it –
but it was the punchline (see what I did there?) to many
of his stories. Most of the tales involved birders who were
misbehaving. Trespassing on a private reserve, selfishly
pushing to the front at a twitch, and – even more heinously
– scaring off a rarity by getting too close with a camera.
Such encounters would have followed much the same script.
Derek speaks in an identifiable – but not 'rustic' – Suffolk
accent. The birder is provocatively silent. Derek shouts: "Oi!
What you doing in there?" Birder, no reaction. "Don't you
know it's private?" No answer. "I am going to ask you to
leave." No response. "I said, I am asking you to leave." Still

no reaction. "I'll ask you one more time. Are you going to leave?" The birder shakes his head and carries on peering through his telescope. So what happened then? Derek: "And then I 'it him!'"

This kind of scenario has been repeated often enough for me to wonder if Derek actually relishes the opportunity for a bit of physical righteous indignation, as it were. Certainly in defence of wildlife, or as a deterrent to those who would harm or abuse it. I like to think of him as Nature's Bodyguard. Indeed, on several occasions he has acted as **my** bodyguard, protecting me from the overzealous attentions of campaigners, Goodies fans, and drunks! He has on at least one occasion, literally picked me up and carried me away from a potentially volatile situation.

Derek is not a dainty man, but he is powerful in both limbs and principles.

In his youth, he played in a rock/soul band, where he sang and tickled the keyboard of a mighty organ, which he protected vehemently from anyone who touched it without asking, even if the upstart was to become one of the world's greatest songwriters, who famously still displays evidence of a close encounter with Derek's fist in the form of an unignorable gap in his front teeth. Is it true? I confess that if it is, I would have expected Ray Davis to have put it in a lyric by now. How about a chorus of: "I was only protecting my organ. And then I 'it him."

Whether or not I am writing about my old friend with appropriate respect I won't know till he reads this. I anticipate a response of: "You cheeky bugger!" He may also be disappointed – or offended – that I have not mentioned his considerable prowess at both cricket and football. I have never seen him play, nor even been involved on the same field, but all I would say is 'I wouldn't want him on the other side!' I can't imagine him either pulling out of a tackle, or bowling slower to the tail-enders! "Well it's a game innit? You wanna win."

Actually, that could be Derek's alternative catchphrase. "I wanna win." Not because he is ultra-competitive or ambitious, but because his beliefs are passionate, his determination is steadfast, and his feelings are deep. Over the years, to me Derek has been a minder, a mentor and a mate. I am happy to say that he is on my team (and vice versa). He is also on Nature's team, and Nature has reason to be grateful.

Bill Oddie, 2013.

Foreword

by Chris Packham

It's about making a difference. Ultimately that's what it's all about. It's not about being right, or clever, or big, or powerful. It's not even about being seen to be the one, or getting the slap on the back or the round of applause, or even being able to say 'I told you so.' It's about having the drive, the energy, the interest and the motivation, the passion to keep trying until you succeed. And the task may be long, or it may be quickly realised. The product may be short-lived or forever long, and the product may be tiny – a peg, a step on which to build – or it may be instantaneously momentous and far reaching. It just doesn't matter. All that ever matters is getting it done, because when all's done it's only the result that counts.

I first met Derek in a sunny field near Santon Downham. I was on the Norfolk side of the river guarding Red-backed Shrikes. Years later I met Derek in a muddy field in Suffolk where we were turning out some hardy equines to manage one of the reserves he was overseeing at the time. We are similar in that we both like doing things. We can do a bit of talking but we think that actions are louder than words, and that without actions we are failing in our duties. We went birding one time in The Netherlands. We had a great weekend, seeing Smew (drakes), Goshawks, Black Woodpeckers and lots of other good stuff. But it felt weird – like skiving, like an indulgence, like nosing around someone else's wildlife when we should have been fixing our own.

Derek has spent a lot of time 'fixing' wildlife and he has done it determinedly. He likes getting on with it. People don't always respect and enjoy this approach – they think it's aggressive, and perhaps they'd rather be having another cappuccino or a flat white, whatever that is. I don't have Derek down as a coffee-morning talker, I have him down as straight-talking top rate conservationist. A bloke who is a good birder but also a bloke blighted by an interest in East Anglian football … Well, if that's his Achilles heel then fair play to him because the rest is spot on. You see Derek Moore is a doer and that is rare and something I aspire to. He is a mentor and a mate. Derek has made a difference and that is why he is a real hero and why it's worth reading this book. Just ignore the bits about Norwich City FC.

Chris Packham, 2013.

1.

From The Womb

Quite a number of years ago I was sitting in an office with colleagues from the printing industry, trying to concentrate on a meeting that was explaining a new accounts system which was being brought in. My attention was waning from the start, but I became even more distracted when I noticed a large bird slowly approaching from over the distant rooftops. Grey Heron first sprang to mind but the adrenalin began pumping as I realized that the bird was holding its neck straight out. By now what was happening in the room was a blur.

I peered hard but could make out no detail, so in sheer panic I rose and excused myself, saying that I needed the bathroom. This was not unusual for me so I hoped nobody suspected my true intentions. I ran downstairs to my car, grabbed my binoculars and was just in time to identify a splendid White Stork heading north. This was a rare sighting, particularly in those days. Satisfied, I hurried back to the meeting room and shuffled into my seat, behaving perfectly normally.

Looking up I realized that everybody was staring at me, some with grins on their faces. The senior member of staff in charge asked: "What was it?" I was rumbled and now they all knew of my obsession. Probably many of them had done so for some time anyway. The fact was, and is, that I could not concentrate on anything else when an interesting bird appeared. So how did this serious malady come about?

I came into this world on 1st January 1943 and over the years I have often been asked when I started birdwatching. My trivial reply is always: "from the womb." I say this because I frankly do not remember. I know from my late mother, my older brother John and my younger sister Janet that I always had an interest in wildlife, and as a toddler was frequently found with caterpillars, frogs and the like in my possession. My mother also told me that I was pointing at birds before I could talk properly and thereafter I always asked what various species were. I know I kept a scrapbook in which I pasted any picture I could find of a bird. This included lots of Christmas cards with various illustrations of European Robins.

Robins were a common image of my childhood because of Christmas cards

I was born in the small market town of Beccles, situated on the River Waveney in Suffolk and therefore right on the border with neighbouring Norfolk. Indeed the town and its river are on the most southerly portion of the Norfolk and Suffolk Broads. It is an attractive town with no special claim to fame except that its unfinished church tower is a landmark for miles around as it rises way above the surrounding marshland. For somebody who was going to grow up as an enthusiastic naturalist then this area is perfect.

My father used to occasionally take the family for walks in the countryside surrounding Beccles. He had a basic knowledge of birds but, never having owned any book on the subject, he often referred to them by their local names.

"There's a Clodbird" (Corn Bunting) or "Look, a King Harry" (European Goldfinch) were the sort of comments I got used to. Father worked for a printing company and humoured my avian interest by one day producing a copy of *The Observer's Book of Birds*. This helped a bit but also added more to my confusion. Every other page had the birds sumptuously displayed in gorgeous colour thanks to Archibald Thorburn's paintings, but in between all the drawings were in black and white. For some time only the species illustrated in colour were definitely on my list. A flock of Bohemian Waxwings I discovered when doing my paper round took several years to identify – I only realised what I had seen once I obtained a book that illustrated and described them well.

My grandmother Moore also inadvertently influenced my early interest in birds. She lived in a small cottage without electricity and with a toilet and washroom across the yard. In her gloomily lit home there stood on the mantelpiece a pair of stuffed King Harrys (European Goldfinches), which she had acquired. Whenever I was there I could barely take my eyes off of those pathetic but beautifully plumaged specimens. Remember I had no binoculars in those days, so pressing my nose up against the glass case was the closest I would get to these superb finches for some years. Grandmother also lived next door to the local rat catcher, a Mr Tubby. For reasons best known to him he kept a pet Eurasian Jay in a small cage. A

My parents with me and my older brother John

great joy for me in those days was to be allowed to go and stare at this unfortunate bird. Two great reasons for looking forward to a visit to grandmother.

Grandmother Moore was also responsible for giving me the best advice of my life, which has subsequently become something of a family motto. After I had grazed my knee in a fall I was wailing away and considering what had been to my mind a near-death experience. Grandmother sagely declared: "If you are scared of dying, boy, you will never live." Wise words indeed.

The other major influence on feeding my passion for birds and other wildlife was my Godfather, Victor Smith, who luckily lived next door to us. He was a keen gardener and spent hours nurturing his prize chrysanthemums. Now and again he would ask me in and we would sit with a copy of a book called *The Countryside Companion*, which had a section on British birds. Illustrated with some of the early photographs of the day, usually all taken at a well-gardened nest, these moments were truly inspiring. One of those early photographers was the late Eric Hosking, but more of him later. Uncle Vic, as we knew him, would point out species he knew well, particularly from his native rural Warwickshire. I am pleased that the book is now in my library.

Growing up in Beccles was a good experience, but perhaps not one that I fully appreciated until later in life. For a start the perception of threats to youngsters was not as great as nowadays. There was little traffic, and in our street for many years there was only one car and that was shared by three brothers. We relied entirely on our bicycles for getting anywhere. The roads were so quiet that full-scale cricket matches went on in our street with little interruption.

It meant that from quite a young age my parents were relaxed about me wandering up to The Dell to look at the rookery, travelling the considerable distance down to Beccles Common or marshes, or cycling out to the many villages around the town. One of my favourite areas was 'The Saints' with its myriad of tiny unspoilt commons covered with lovely ponds and wild flowers. Here, with hastily dug up worm and a piece of wool, you could catch lots of the now very protected Great Crested Newts. Quite a few of these splendid amphibians ended up living in a large aquarium in my parents' cramped conservatory.

There were many bird species in these areas too, as we had not yet seen the mass destruction of hedgerows and woodlands. Yellowhammers sang from every possible corner and were taken very much for granted. Grey Partridges were a common sight and Red-legged Partridges then much rarer. Little Owls were easy to find in pollarded willows and oaks and Tree Sparrows in mature stands of parkland trees. What's more, Turtle Doves were a common summer visitor and their soporific purring a real sound of warmer days. These were idyllic times.

With my sister Janet at a very early age

In later years I took up coarse fishing, which was merely an excuse for sitting for long hours by the River Waveney and the chance to see more birds. You could rent a rowing boat in those days to get you to good fishing points. Here, moored up against a stand of phragmites reeds, I would sometimes look for Reed Warblers' nests and I remember being highly impressed by these intricately woven structures.

I also really enjoyed our annual family holiday in those days, which constituted staying either with Grandmother Brown or Aunt Jessie and Uncle Frank in my mother's home town of Colchester, just across the county border in Essex. My father was very canny and always arranged the event to coincide with the Colchester Cricket Week. One year I remember getting to Castle Park early with my father and brother, and I do not know how Dad managed it but I know we met players from the Yorkshire and Lancashire teams because my brother and I had their autographs in a book. These included such giants of the day as Len Hutton, Norman Yardley, Johnny Wardle, Doug Insole, Trevor Bailey, Cyril Washbrook and Brian Statham. What a thrill that was to us boys. I also remember being in a Colchester pub garden when my father emerged with a large but friendly youngish man. The man pressed a large, impressive medal into my hand and I wondered why. Then father explained that this man was Vic Keeble and he played for Newcastle United, and what I was holding was his 1955 FA Cup Winner's

Medal won a week or two previously in the Wembley final against Manchester City. I could not wait to get back to school to share that one with my mates.

When our family was on holiday in north Essex we would sometimes take a day trip to Brightlingsea or Walton on the Naze. My mother was not keen on these excursions because there was little or no beach in these places, only lots of glorious estuarine mud. I was of course delighted and spent hours stalking Eurasian Oystercatchers, Ruddy Turnstones, Eurasian Curlews and much more. I would get really filthy, much to everyones' annoyance, but I simply couldn't resist another chance of following my obsession.

These were very early days and I was still at primary school, with little hope of widening my knowledge of birds. The big move forward occurred when I passed the then Eleven Plus exam and moved on to the Sir John Leman Grammar School, again in Beccles. It was not long before a chance encounter started to open up a form of birdwatching. Teachers often used to sit at the head of tables at lunch and on one occasion as I rose I dropped my satchel and out tipped my *Observer's Book of Birds*. The master was the formidable G.B.G. Benson, or as I later learned Chris to his friends. Picking up the book he smiled and asked me to see him after school.

I was more than a bit nervous as I waited outside the staff room at 3.45pm that afternoon. Mr Benson always

The author aged 10

wore thick tweed suits and sported a military moustache. He was a formidable figure and carried an aura of authority. I was astonished when he told me he was something called an ornithologist and that he would be glad to show me birds both in the school grounds and, if my parents gave permission, around his beloved Southwold. He also told me that he represented something called the BTO in Suffolk. I was thrilled to be offered this chance, if a bit nervous. I had always warmed to Mr Benson ever since I had seen him hit a massive six in the staff versus school cricket match.

There began a great but unlikely friendship, and it proved to be a seminal moment in my life. Mr Benson took me round Beccles Cemetery after school, pointing out all the common birds, and later (aged about 12) I was allowed to cycle the nine miles to Blythburgh, where I would meet him and we would walk around the Blyth Estuary. What wonders appeared here. Flocks of noisy Common Shelducks, piping Common Redshanks and the haunting cries of Eurasian Curlews. A real treat was to be taken to Walberswick and walk around the Blois estate. Mr Benson was on good terms with Sir Gervase Blois and we were allowed to wander at will. This was long before the area became a National Nature Reserve and I was introduced to Marsh Harriers, Eurasian Bitterns, Woodlarks, Red-backed Shrikes, Bearded Tits and many more species.

He also took me along to The Dingle Bird Club where I

Bitterns were a big part of my Suffolk birding

was able to see birds caught and small metal rings attached to their legs so that their movements could be traced. This activity really captivated a young schoolboy and was to feature quite a bit in later years. It was here that I met others of my own age and most memorable was meeting David Pearson, who was at Leiston Grammar School at the time. I can remember him and Peter Smith playing cricket against me at school and them chatting in the slips, telling me of good birds just as their giant fast bowler was in his final stride. They knew how to get me out alright.

My kind schoolmaster did much more than just introduce me to birds. He produced my first copy of

Peterson's *A Field Guide to the Birds of Britain and Europe* and introduced me at too early an age to Adnams Bitter beer and how to use a soft tweed trilby to protect one's testicles when getting over a barbed wire fence.

I would be engaged to be married when Mr Benson (I could never bring myself to call him Chris) died and I felt obliged to take on his mantle as BTO representative for Suffolk. The memory of those wonderful times stays with me to this day. With all the political correctness and health and safety issues would such a liaison be possible today?

During those early years it was obvious that I needed binoculars. My father was not convinced, at least I thought he wasn't until he appeared one day with a small pair of 8x40s, but with the annoying feature of having a cross in the middle of the view. That meant every bird had this cross superimposed on its body. They were obviously intended for use by the military but they sufficed until I was able to buy my own.

At this time I followed my interest in birds by visiting places on my bike, and often with my mongrel Judy. Beccles Common was a great magnet with its heathy grassland, gorse and rudimentary golf course. Here Common Linnets, Yellowhammers, Green Woodpeckers and even the occasional Common Nightingale emerged from the pages of my books. Beccles Marshes were even more revealing. Before the days of drainage and agricultural improvement they were a haven.

Nightingales singing at Beccles Common were one of the pleasures of my younger days

Nesting Common Snipe, Common Redshank and Northern Lapwing frequented the grassland and Sedge and Reed Warblers the dykes. Common Cuckoo and Turtle Dove were numerous in those days. The real paradise was Beccles Sewage Farm, a seemingly vast area of sludge lagoons and a small flooded marsh with lots of fallen trees. The latter housed a small colony of Black-headed Gulls and the former could be full of waders at migration time. These included Green Sandpiper, Common Greenshank, Spotted Redshank and Dunlin. Goodness knows what I missed there through lack of knowledge. Over the years I saw both my first Peregrine Falcon and Osprey in this area. I also managed to fall into one of the sludge lagoons once, but luckily I only went in up

The gentle purring of Turtle Doves was a common sound of summer in my youth

to my waste. I was hosed down by my mother on my return home and she threw my clothes away.

Recent trips to Beccles show that much has changed. The common is still there and its golf course, but many of the marshes have been drained and turned into sports pitches. There is a bypass between the common and other marshes and a Morrisons supermarket stands on the site of my beloved sludge lagoons.

As I grew older my trusty bike enabled me to get a bit further and take in even better marshes at North Cove and Barnby. Life was bit more difficult here because many of the marshes were private and it was not unusual for me to be chased off by landowners. I took little notice and kept going back and learning how to hide from their view.

During summer large numbers of cattle used to be brought down to Beccles and fattened on the marshes. I used to meet adults who were carrying binoculars and assumed I had found some kindred spirits. This was not entirely true as they were marsh men and their job was to regularly count the cattle in their charge. They did have considerable knowledge of the marshes and their wildlife though and often teased me, but I suspect they were impressed with my energy in searching out my quarry.

Schooldays fairly leapt by. I was not a great scholar and proved to be a bit of a trial to both my parents and some of the teachers. I was already extremely keen on sport and could not see why I would never be able to earn a living as a footballer or cricketer. I was quite good at both games but nowhere near good enough. Because of this, more academic subjects were largely ignored. I did like woodwork and technical drawing but our draconian headmaster of the day decided that I should take Latin instead. My father interjected on my behalf but was told I had something called "Oxbridge potential" and therefore Latin was essential. My reaction to this was to always put my name on the top of any exam paper and then go into a mental trance for the duration, thinking of all the wonderful creatures I was now seeing on TV programmes presented by Peter Scott, David Attenborough, Hans and Lotte Hass and Armand and Michaela Denis. Needless to say I achieved an extraordinary set of 0 per cent marks for that subject. This, of course, could not go unpunished and I was eventually moved from the elitist A-stream to the more mundane B-stream.

Schooldays then were unrecognisable from today. I was punished for eating an ice cream in school uniform. The fact that I was with my mother, who had bought me the ice cream, made no difference. I saw one boy sent home from a school football match because he was not wearing his regulation grey trousers with his blazer. The draconian staff never realised that his mother was washing his school greys at the weekend. There was so much petty discipline that you would have thought we were in the army. There was little to no formal communication between the school and parents, in complete contrast to what happened with my own children. Although I am sure that the pompous headmaster, who was keen on doing a little social climbing, would talk to the parents he favoured, and probably at Rotary Club or in the Conservative Club.

I have to say that, although I was obviously not a model pupil, some of my teachers were fantastic people and over the years became good friends. Our sports master David Stewart was exceptional and such a good motivator of young people. He encouraged everyone whatever their ability and showed his human touch by getting a whole bunch of us a day off from school so we could watch Norwich City play Luton Town in a FA Cup semi-final replay in 1959. Sadly if he were teaching today he would probably be fired for being politically incorrect. He was a passionate Scotsman with a great sense of humour and he loved his sport. He excelled even in my day as a cricketer and always treated us boys as friends, giving us nicknames rather than always addressing us as though we were in army. George Ford was our biology master and his wife Pam was the girls' PE teacher. They too showed their exceptional human side by befriending pupils as well as having a huge influence on our lives. They have remained friends all my life and travelled with me on some of my wildlife tours to far flung corners of the world. Sadly George passed away a year or two ago but Pam and I still keep in touch.

My schooldays ended in the fifth year (known as Year 11 these days) and I find it hard even now to forgive my school, and especially the headmaster, for how it all ended. On the last day of term in 1958 many of my colleagues were congratulating themselves on achieving the necessary O-Levels to return to the sixth form. That left a number of us in limbo and assuming we had to leave. Nobody said a word to us so we went home wondering what was next.

Most working class parents in the years following the Second World War were anxious to see their children in employment as soon as possible and mine were no exception. I was encouraged to interview and accept a job in a local bank, which would be considered a most respectable choice.

The bank required me to provide a reference from the school so I went to see the headmaster. He expressed great surprise that I was taking a job and informed me that I was expected back at school to sit two O-Levels and then join the sixth form and take part in the quest for university. That was the first I had ever heard of this and he did not put up much of a struggle, so I guess he was glad to see the back of a pupil who was such a rebel. Even when I met him again in his 90s he did not seem to easily acknowledge what I had by then achieved. I did not fit his vision of one of his successes. After all I had left school with three O-Levels and had not achieved a university place. In his eyes without that you could not possibly do anything worthwhile. He asked me what I was doing, even though he was a member of the Suffolk Wildlife Trust and I had been its Director for more than a decade. I am sure he considered me a failure.

It was a sad end to my schooldays, although quite a lot of it was my own fault.

2.

After Fledging

So now I was in the adult world, or so I thought. I had a job in a bank in Beccles which at first I quite liked. I was always happy talking to people and the interface with customers was to my liking. On quiet days I would still be thinking of birds and how I could turn more of those images in my books into reality. What I needed was transport. I started by saving a little of my weekly wages of just over £2 and decided to get myself a moped. It was a 50cc NSU Quickly (nowadays that name would be reason to sue under the Trade Descriptions Act), which just about got up to 30mph with a following wind.

This purchase or hire purchase enabled me to explore a

bit more. I was able to get to Blythburgh and Walberswick on my own terms and in my own time. I still did not have regular contact with anyone else interested in birds (except Mr Benson) so I was very much a loner. I did begin to find more birds for myself and soon appreciated what a good place the Suffolk coast was. I made an expedition into Norfolk to Fritton Lake and trespassed into the surrounding woods to gaze at my first Great Crested Grebes. This was a scarce species in those days and how was I to know that soon it would become far more numerous.

In 1953 the first Collared Doves appeared in north Norfolk and I found the first for Beccles on the Police Station TV aerial in 1956. This was a great rarity in those days but it very quickly spread and soon was a common sight everywhere. Nevertheless it was a significant moment in British ornithology and was mirrored by later colonisations by the likes of Cetti's Warbler and Little Egret which followed in later decades.

Life was now good and as I progressed at work I was allowed to go on staff relief duty at Bungay and Harleston. Going to Harleston meant I had to journey west along the Waveney Valley where, from the bus, it was possible to see a scarce bird of the day which nested in the marshes. It was so exciting to see the black-and-white heads of Canada Geese sticking up from the grass and reeds. I did not care much that this was a feral species, with this population having

The Little Egret was formerly a great rarity in this country, but it has now successfully colonised many parts of the UK

originated at nearby Redgrave Lake, and I proudly added it to my growing list.

I also used to explore the Bungay area a bit. I do remember that there always seemed to be a nesting pair of Grey Wagtails at the back of the town on a small stream. This was a very uncommon bird in East Anglia in those days. The Bath Hills on the Norfolk side of the Waveney were also worth a look, and in those days Red Squirrels still occurred there. And Broome Heath had a pair or two of nesting Red-backed Shrikes.

Having achieved a meagre income and the moped I turned my attention to binoculars. There was not much choice in those days and I soon became the proud owner of some Swift 10x40s purchased from our local camera shop. Thank goodness the cross had gone. This really opened up my eyes and I was able to see birds better and also realise some of my mistakes. How could I have possibly mistaken a Lesser Whitethroat for a rare Marsh Warbler.

I continued to play sport at weekends, in between birding expeditions and of course work. My obsession was growing. Concentrating on anything but birds was a challenge. Playing cricket for Beccles, one of the team was David Frost (now Sir David Frost) and he was already dabbling in the media with Anglia TV. He learned of my sorties into Beccles Sewage Works and asked me lots of questions and also the names of some birds. A few nights later he did a hilarious stand up piece filmed at the sewage ponds about some nutcase chasing around looking for strangely named birds amongst the public excreta of Beccles. I was flattered.

I had now got into the habit of collecting things. I scoured second-hand bookshops for anything on birds. I went to Beccles Library, where they had very little. I took out a large copy of *Audubon's Birds of North America* on more-or-less permanent loan and spent many hours looking at exotic creatures I knew I would never see. The book became so dog-eared with my use that after about a year the Librarian told me to keep it. Over the years my library has grown and grown. I could never resist any book on birds

The author in his cricketing days, looking rather Bothamesque!

and now it is a real challenge to find room for everything I have accumulated.

I also fell in love with those cases of stuffed birds that the Victorians so loved. I begged them from friends and relatives – yes, I already had Grandmother Moore's King Harries and occasionally bought additions to my collection at local sales rooms. A local *Beccles and Bungay Journal* reporter heard of this weird fascination with dead birds and did a piece on me one week. The next week I was receiving offers of lots more stuffed birds. Soon the walls of my bedroom were stacked high with cases containing everything from Eurasian Curlew to Hen Harrier. Now I was able to study the specimens of some scarce species in close-up. I was the only person in the house thrilled by my new collection. I was also beginning to take an interest in the opposite sex and I was convinced that "Come up and see my stuffed birds" was much more alluring than "Come up and see my etchings."

Eventually most of these stuffed birds went to a local pub, where they remained on display for years. I still have a Corncrake and a splendid male Hen Harrier. I, of course, am glad that the fashion of making a decoration of dead wild birds is now mostly gone. With so many talented artists at large it is now more gratifying to collect works of art which represent our wildlife so well.

Mr Benson had taken me many times to the now defunct Buss Creek Marsh in Southwold. It was a gem of a place, being so small that many birds were very concentrated in a tiny area. Benson had once found three Marsh Sandpipers here so it was worth close scrutiny. Regular visits enabled me to see my first Spoonbill, Black Terns, Wood Sandpiper and Temminck's Stint here. It is very sad that this fantastic site has been drained and has therefore lost most of its avian interest. One day I met another person carrying not binoculars, but a monocular. He declared at once that he was not really a birdwatcher but a botanist, but admitted that he did quite like my flying friends. His name was Charles Bastard and that day he tried persuading me to consider joining the Lowestoft Field Club. It took a few more years for me to follow his advice.

Walberswick was still a major magnet for me and I went there as often as I could. The site was still not a nature reserve then, but it was riddled with footpaths and once you had made friends with Jack List, the local gamekeeper, all would be well. Jack was a tiny man whose gun was almost taller than him, and he had a loveable springer spaniel called Crunch. He lived in a tiny cottage by the road that led up to Westwood Lodge. Jack loved to chat to the local birders and he was not backward in admitting that Marsh Harriers were no friends of his. The RSPB used to hand out a cash payment for successful nests in those days, and that enabled a truce to be declared between these rare birds and people like Jack.

Talking to Jack was a pleasure. He was a real Suffolk man,

always staying close to his roots. He was born in that tiny cottage and died there too. I remember going in to see him one day whilst he was listening to an Ipswich Town football match on the radio. He was entranced and quite tense until the end of the game. I asked Jack if he went to watch Ipswich play at Portman Road. "No" he said "I have never been to Ipswich. I went to Halesworth (ten miles away) once to have a medical for the war. Apparently my feet were no good so I failed. I have never been away from here since".

He became a good acquaintance and I learned a great deal about the countryside and its wildlife from this little man.

By now I was a member of the RSPB and I was anxious to visit the mythical Minsmere. It was so difficult then. You could not just go on a whim whenever there was good weather or north-easterly winds. No, you had to write to a grand-named address called The Lodge somewhere far to the west and ask for a permit. I decided against doing this until I had met somebody who had done it. It all sounded a bit nerve-wracking. So it would be a few more years before I got there.

I had discovered Benacre and Covehithe, which were a bit closer to home, and I liked the place because there were so few people there. I became uncontrollable with excitement at the discovery of my first male Smew. What a marvellous bird and I still get a great kick whenever I see this species. Winter was very good at Benacre with regular great flocks of tinkling Snow Buntings and scarce seaduck,

Bearded Tits breed regularly in Suffolk's reedbeds

grebes and divers turning up at the gravel pits.

In summer Little Terns came to nest on the beach and Eurasian Bitterns, Bearded Tits and Marsh Harriers bred in the reedbeds. The site was also extremely good for migrants and worth checking as often as possible in spring and autumn. The rewards were great with regular sightings of Wrynecks, Icterine Warblers and Red-backed Shrikes in autumn. Even scarcer species like Barred Warbler and European Serin were also seen more than once. In August 1968, driving past Covehithe Church, I nearly ran over a strange bird in the road. Following the creature into the churchyard I could not believe my eyes as I was gazing at my first-ever Spotted Nutcracker, which was part of a huge influx of that species into the UK that year.

In 1982 nearby Kessingland gained fame as the location of Britain's first and only White-crowned Wheatear, which was photographed and identified by Brian Brown. Many Suffolk birders dipped out on this bird. Many from the Ipswich area were in Scotland but perversely their wives, girlfriends and children all went to see the wheatear just so they could tell them what they missed. I too missed the bird as it was found on the Friday evening and Saturday morning was my turn to cut the wicket for our afternoon cricket match. It was gone by Sunday.

Back in the 1960s I rarely saw any other people at Benacre, let alone other birdwatchers. It was idyllic and I learned so much by myself just through looking at everything, keeping notes and identifying as much as possible. The Benacre Estate was very tolerant of me and on request issued me with a letter which gave me free access to all the interesting land they owned. In return I produced a little report of what I had seen and the people running the estate seemed genuinely interested in this.

Here again I made a friend of a local gamekeeper, Ted Fountain. Ted was a West Country man but again he had an extraordinary knowledge of the countryside and local wildlife. He called me once to go and see a migrant Golden Oriole in his garden. I remember going home with my bag full of his home-grown vegetables. The other great help to me on the Benacre Estate was Jim Good, the manager of the pig unit at Covehithe. I used to wander around that area when Eurasian Stone-curlews nested on the more heathy fields and Hawfinches were a regular sight.

It was about this time that I read in the newspaper of a great rarity called a Houbara Bustard (which has now been 'split' as Macqueen's Bustard) at somewhere called Westleton. I read the article with great interest and admired the photograph taken by Eric Hosking, but decided it was too far to go in very cold weather on a moped. How different things are today, and by the way I have still never seen this species anywhere in the world.

I was getting about a bit more now as I had changed the moped for a Vespa 125 scooter. This could reach heady speeds up to 60mph and meant I could go further. It also enabled me to start to socialise and go out with my pals. It was one of many sorties into Lowestoft that brought the greatest fortune in my life when, just before my 19th birthday, I met Beryl Saunders. Now she was quite a sportswoman and excelled at swimming, having been the Suffolk Women's Breaststroke champion on more than one occasion. She therefore was happy that I was playing table tennis, football and cricket. However, she made it quite clear that she would have preferred me to play rugby and to this day it is one of her favourite sports. What she would

At last, decent transport to get me to the birds

think of my interest in birds lay heavy in those days and I bided my time to spring my surprise on her.

By then Minsmere was slightly more accessible and one evening after cricket I whisked her down to the Island Mere Hide as I had heard that a Eurasian Spoonbill was present. Such a spectacular bird was bound to impress. When we entered the hide there were two obvious problems which might undermine my cunning plan. First, the spoonbill was present but fast asleep on one leg and with its spatulate bill tucked under its wing. Second, in the hide was John Denney, a most eccentric and aged volunteer who was obsessed with Marsh Harriers. As usual John did not look up but immediately bellowed "Marsh Harrier" and began

Beryl's first Eurasian Spoonbill stayed asleep all evening

his commentary on two birds about to make a spectacular food pass right in front of the hide. Beryl was very impressed with what she saw and not in the least put off by John or indeed me.

By now there was another threat to my obsession. A sporting pal, Dick Brand, had acquired a set of drums from an uncle. I played the piano very badly and he invited me to busk along to his efforts at drumming. After a while he introduced Graham West, who played the guitar as badly as I did the piano. I suddenly realised Dick was serious about turning us into a band. A very competent guitarist, John 'Spike' Taylor, was added, along with a bass guitarist in David West. As I had been in the church choir as a kid I was told to give up the piano and become lead singer. This meant we started life performing free at harvest suppers, village hall events, and the like.

Within a year we were actually quite proficient at reproducing cover versions of The Beatles and Chuck Berry numbers and Dick was on a mission. Graham was cruelly sacked and replaced by Brian Wilson (not the guy from The Beach Boys) and we marched on. We began playing at youth clubs and were being paid. Better equipment was purchased with enormous support from Dick's father and we also acquired a battered bus.

After appearing on a version of Hughie Green's *Opportunity Knocks* on the Wellington Pier in Great Yarmouth things got very serious. We started playing regularly at holiday camps in Caister-on-Sea and Hopton, and also at the Garibaldi Ballroom in Great Yarmouth. In those days we were known as the Blackjacks. Ambition drove us forward and David West decided to call it a day. He was replaced by Lionel Knights. We also added John Tuttle on tenor saxophone and Keith Hart on baritone saxophone and changed our name from Blackjacks to The Style and later the Soul Concern. Our style changed from pure pop to soul, blues and Tamla Motown.

In a period of nine years we had become a popular local and support band appearing with many of the stars of the day. We played at gigs throughout East Anglia and the East

The author at the keyboard with colleagues from The Style

Midlands and occasionally in London. We were fortunate
to share the bill with The Kinks, Marmalade, Alan Price,
Georgie Fame, Geno Washington and the Ram Jam Band,
The Who and many more. We also appeared as a resident
band for pirate radio station Radio London, playing at their
Saturday night roadshows up and down the country, and we
were invited to do some recording. This part-time activity
had serious implications for my birding. The rest of the band
was bemused at best by my need to see birds everywhere.
They did get immensely frustrated when I insisted on
stopping en route to gigs to see a bird. We played a lot on the
north Norfolk coast and that was most convenient for me.

My life was now full (too full) of major distractions from

birds, which I guess was a result of me growing up and trying to do normal things, but also keeping the birds going.

It was at this time that a major disaster struck our family. My father was diagnosed with bowel cancer at the age of 59 and after surgery and a year of hope he sadly died. I was only 18 and it was a huge wrench for my mother and the family to cope with his loss. After a year or so my mother married again to Rowley and we all moved on.

3.

Pairing Up

In December 1964 Beryl and I married and set up home in Carlton Colville, Suffolk. It was here that another major moment occurred in my passion for birds. I noticed a large man walk past my house sporting binoculars at roughly the same time each day. At the earliest opportunity I intercepted him, and after a cheery hello asked if he was a birdwatcher. His brusque reply of "What's it got to do with you" was somewhat unexpected. However, for those that knew him well this was Brian Brown and I had got him on one of his good days.

It turned out that Brian lived just up the road from me and what is more he was a regular weekend volunteer at

Brian and Christine Brown – Brian was my first birding pal

Minsmere RSPB reserve. He said that if I knew what was good for me I should join him on his forays to help at the reserve. This was the point at which I had finally found a kindred spirit and somebody to actually go birding with. I jumped at the chance to help out at Minsmere, and for the next few years I accompanied Brian and Dick Briggs to this paradise for birds and took part in activities to build the Scrape. This meant that I came into contact with Herbert (Bert) Axell, the charismatic warden of Minsmere.

Bert was an impressive, self-opinionated, obsessive and extremely driven man. His vision at Minsmere was easy to follow. He could see the potential for even more birds than already occurred and set about achieving this by some of the earliest habitat-creation schemes in the UK, which included the famous Scrape. I was inspired, and this convinced me that there was more to birds than just seeing them. You had to work and fight to make sure they had suitable habitat to survive. This set me off on a new path in my quest for birds.

Minsmere was also a great place to meet many of the birding celebrities of that time. I really enjoyed assisting Eric Hosking in carrying his gear down to the photographic hide. Eric was one of the world's true gentlemen, who always had time to discuss the birds he was after. Sadly, today many people take photographs but do not bother to learn much about their subject in the way that Eric did. How stimulating it was to sit chatting with Dr David Lack about bird science and conservation. He treated me as an equal and encouraged me to investigate my thoughts. There were many more, including a brief exchange with Roger Tory Peterson – an encounter that left me so speechless I forgot to get him to autograph my copy of his field guide.

These were some of the best days of my birding life. We would assemble at dawn at weekends and, having put up a few mist nets, discover what was about. We would check from the hides and then devote the rest of the day (or morning) to working on the Scrape. This would involve laying down plastic farm sacks on mud islands and then bringing barrow-loads of shingle to cover the plastic. This was gruelling work, but worth it to see the spectacular

Upland Sandpiper was a species later removed from Bert Axell's list of Minsmere rarities

results. I usually had to disappear at lunchtime to go off and
play football or cricket.

In those days we were pleased just to watch the birds at
Minsmere. That was not to say we did not appreciate the
unusual and rare. Throughout the seasons there were always
good birds to see. Marsh Harriers were so rare then that
in 1971 the only pair nesting in the UK was at Minsmere.
These birds were treasured and protected, and from this pair
the population eventually was able to increase to the healthier
level it is at today.

This was the time when Bert caught a wader which he was
adamant was a Red-necked Stint – a mainly Asian species
that had not yet been recorded in the UK. We were quite

naive then and thought that if Bert said so then it must be one. I never saw the bird in the hand, only feeding on the scrape, and I had no reason to quiz Bert either way. Anyway, the British Birds Rarities Committee did not accept his identification, which does sound strange considering that he had the bird in his hand. There were people about in those days who reckoned that Bert was getting careless in his quest to record as many species as possible at Minsmere. Indeed, since his death the very questionable spring Pechora Pipit and an equally suspect Upland Sandpiper have been removed from the records. To be fair, at that time we did not have the literature or experience that the thousands of birders have today. One of the most experienced Suffolk birders, Gerald Jobson, did admit that he was certain the Pechora Pipit ID was not correct but kept quiet, because if he had expressed a negative opinion then Bert would have never have let him in to Minsmere again.

He was probably correct about Bert. Another great Suffolk birder, Kerry Cobb, was also always at Minsmère with his wife, Audrey. However, I arrived one day to be told by Bert that he had banned Kerry from the reserve for something so trivial that I cannot recall the reason today. This seemed very draconian and more of a loss to the reserve than anything else. There is no doubt that Bert was a bully. He once tried that tactic on me but my reaction was not what he expected. He backed off and we really were friends

Herbert Axell MBE surveying his Minsmere empire

to the end. Of course, it did not occur to anyone in those days that Bert may not actually have the authority to ban anyone. Surely that could not happen in the 21st century?

I do remember one day when small groups of birders were walking down the beach towards Sizewell. I asked Bert Axell what was going on. He revealed that a Trumpeter Finch – a bird from desert lands – had been found near the power station, but in his opinion this was obviously an escape and not worth the effort. I took his advice and carried on working on a very muddy island. Now, of course, we all know that this was accepted as a wild bird and the first for Suffolk. I have now seen this species in Jordan but never in the UK.

Brian and I used to find a few rarities on the reserve. We were persuaded to write up our descriptions and hand them to Bert and we assumed that he would pass them on to the rarities committee. It was just a little galling to find out later that these records would always be published as 'H.E. Axell, P.J. Makepeace, *et al*.' Michael Seago from Norfolk always called me *et al* for the rest of his life.

Minsmere was the vision of one man. And Bert was a difficult man who suffered fools not at all. He could be charming one moment and rude and pompous only minutes later. He made many enemies as well as having influential friends. His wife Joan (or 'The Rear Axell', as named by the late Tony Marshall) was the driving force behind Bert and the two ruled Minsmere with a set of their own moral and authoritarian standards. Joan even once banned a young lady volunteer for hanging her smalls on a linen line in clear view of her husband's office. Bert's vision and work set the scene for emerging conservationists everywhere. Many visited Minsmere to see what Bert was doing and he himself went round the world talking about his work. Now it is possible to see 'Scrapes' in different countries all over the planet.

On reflection I suppose that if Bert had not been so single minded, so obsessed and so resourceful then Minsmere may never have happened. He did not rely on anybody else and he just kept at it until his vision was achieved. Maybe these qualities are what is missing today in redressing the balance in favour of wildlife.

The shame for the RSPB is that those in charge at the time of Bert's retirement, and at the time of his death, did not see fit to recognise his work in any way. There is still nothing at Minsmere to acknowledge that this place might not have existed without the efforts of Herbert Axell MBE. I hope that something will be done in the future as it would be churlish not to recognise the enormous contribution made by this man.

By now Brian Brown was my constant birding companion and he introduced me to many good areas in north Suffolk and south Norfolk. He was also a stalwart of the Lowestoft Field Club, which I eventually joined. I did get frustrated when evening meetings would be taken up with long discussions on botanical issues, but a big plus was meeting characters such as Fred Cook, Harold Jenner, Jim Warner and Jimmy Read. They were all very experienced naturalists and I learnt so much talking and listening to them.

It was Brian who first suggested that we and our wives, and later our children, might start taking some holidays together. Well we did and I can recall memorable first visits to Wales and Scotland. I can also recall on one occasion Brian and I were creeping about in Abernethy Forest on Speyside when we came across a thin piece of wire running low through the undergrowth. We beat a hasty retreat as we were convinced we had almost bumped into a warning system for those guarding the Osprey nest at Loch Garten. We didn't fancy feeling the heavy hand of the RSPB on our collars.

Brian and sometimes Dick Briggs were inspirational friends as I set out on my quest for birds, and it is a great sadness to me that neither is still alive today. Dick was a keen ringer in my early days and I was sometimes allowed to accompany him during his sessions at Carlton Marshes. It was with Dick that I first obtained a proper BTO ringing permit and began to learn more. I cannot forget how Dick came to my house one night and interrupted my misery as I lay in bed with influenza, or whatever it is that men get. Since I lived within five minutes of the marsh and he knew that I had never ringed a Jack Snipe, he brought one round for me to do. This I did shaking with excitement, and Dick promptly took the bird back and released it onto the marsh, so it was all done in about 30 minutes. Our obsession knew no bounds.

We shall probably never know why Dick was sadly found drowned in his beloved Oulton Broad many years later, but I shall always remember the great moments we had together. He was another self-taught naturalist and, together with his old father, spent years helping out with a number of nature conservation projects.

It was around this time, on 5th September 1965 to be

precise, that a major ornithological event took place on the Suffolk coast. Weather conditions were precisely right for a huge 'fall' of migrants. Light rain occurred on a night when enormous numbers of the passerines which had bred in Scandinavia were heading south off the coast of East Anglia. Their vision suddenly impaired, thousands of birds were forced down into a small area of coastal East Anglia. The fall occurred roughly from Lowestoft to Ipswich, in a narrow belt east of the A12.

I awoke that morning thinking about my cricket match later in the day and opened the bedroom curtains. To my amazement there was a Pied Flycatcher on our clothes line, and then another and another. I walked outside and counted a total of 17 in the garden. This was very unusual. There was little passing of information in those days so I did not know what others were experiencing. I went down to our fish and chip shop for some lunch and noted Whinchats and Common Redstarts everywhere. They were not just in typical habitat, but also in the gutters and even in the middle of the road.

I arrived at Lowestoft's Denes Oval cricket ground just before 2pm and was immediately called by Sid the groundsman. He described how, when he was cutting the wicket in the late morning, he saw what he thought was smoke coming onto the ground from the beach area. To his amazement the smoke turned out to be flocks of small

Whinchats featured heavily in the 'Great Fall'

birds, some of which landed on the pitch. Sadly a number of these succumbed very quickly. Knowing my interest, Sid had collected up both dead and weakened birds and put them in a cardboard box and warmed the living ones by his boiler.

Imagine the joy of taking dozens of Common Redstarts, Whinchats, Pied Flycatchers and other less common species and warming them in my hands before releasing them into the shrubbery behind the pavilion. When the match started we were fielding first and I concocted a tale for the captain, saying that I was feeling a bit queasy and could I field on the boundary instead of at my usual second slip. This achieved, I spent two hours on the fringe of the field with Wrynecks, an Ortolan Bunting, Bluethroat and many commoner species, while pretending to note what was happening in the middle. I cannot remember anything about the cricket on that day but I will never forget what a spectacle I had witnessed. Next day all the birds had disappeared and now I was hearing news from a few other people of what they had seen of what was to become known as the 'Great Fall'. One cannot help thinking that the populations of most of these species have become so reduced in recent decades that they could not occur in such numbers ever again.

Our married life was progressing well and all this time I was working first for Birds Eye at Lowestoft and later for the printers William Clowes at Great Yarmouth and Beccles. In my Birds Eye days my thirst for birds was satisfied by checking out the UK's most easterly location, Ness Point, and the harbour a short distance from my office. Purple Sandpipers regularly wintered in the area and the fish docks attracted Glaucous and Iceland Gulls in good numbers. Migrants were also seen, including Bohemian Waxwings feeding on ornamental berries around the Birds Eye factory and once a Wryneck in the staff cycle shed. It was in this area that my pal Brian Brown found a Franklin's Gull in 1977 and I saw Suffolk's first Cory's Shearwater in 1974.

In Great Yarmouth I discovered the joys of Breydon Water, especially the area around Burgh Castle, during my lunch hours. A few Eurasian White-fronted Geese were still frequenting these marshes in winter, as well as small numbers of Bewick's Swans. It was here that I got to know local ornithologists Peter Allard and the late Percy Trett. Peter once turned up at my office with a Cory's Shearwater in a cardboard box. He had received the bird exhausted and was now ready to release it back into the wild. I must confess here that part of my obsession was with seeing birds in my beloved Suffolk. It was therefore a bit annoying to find a Red-necked Grebe at Burgh Castle which was keeping well to the north of the channel in the River Waveney, placing it well inside the Norfolk boundary. My cricketing ability meant that a few well-judged stones hurled across the river ensured the hapless bird quickly swam south and became a Suffolk record.

On wet and draughty days I discovered that in winter small rafts of seaduck were often to be found off the sandstone cliffs at Gorleston and Hopton. I would sit here on cold days and point my old brass telescope out of the car window. I soon realised that small numbers of Common and Velvet Scoters could be seen regularly, as well as a small group of Long-tailed Ducks. Indeed I counted 102 Velvet Scoters there in November 1972 and I wonder if they and the other species are still found there on a regular basis.

Because I was finding birds in Norfolk now, I often spoke to Michael Seago who served his county as bird recorder for over 30 years. Knowing that I often looked around Yarmouth during my lunch hour he asked me if I would kindly let him know the names and numbers of Russian wood boats at

Jewsons Timber Merchants in the harbour. I never dared ask why but wondered if he worked for MI5 in his spare time. This was during the height of the Cold War and maybe my imagination got the better of me.

Later and somewhat conveniently I transferred to the Beccles office of William Clowes, which was a bit closer to home. Beccles was my home town, of course, and I was able to return to the marshes for a regular lunchtime walk, but already they were degrading as far as wildlife was concerned.

By now my involvement with birds was accelerating. I had taken on the responsibility of being regional representative for the British Trust for Ornithology, which meant that I was the local contact for members and also had to organise national surveys at a local level. It was not an onerous job and enabled me to extend my contacts in Suffolk and also with professional ornithologists and the BTO's headquarters, which in those days was in Tring, Hertfordshire.

It was carrying out atlas work for the BTO that once again showed me how interested large landowners could be in such projects. I approached Lord Somerleyton, who owned a large area of north-east Suffolk including some splendid areas of habitat. He was most co-operative and through his gamekeepers gave me complete access for the survey. Many years later when we met again through Suffolk Wildlife Trust business he still remembered that early survey and continued to be mindful of nature conservation on his estate.

This job kept me busy and made me feel that I was making a real contribution to birds. Dick Briggs, one of my constant companions during the Minsmere days, made me aware of an organisation called the Suffolk Trust for Nature Conservation, which was buying an area of marshes at Carlton Colville. This initiative was being promoted by the enormously popular and eccentric naturalist Ted Ellis. Dick was taking on a role there as Voluntary Warden and enlisted me as one of his assistants. Our main interest in the early days was a nesting pair of Montagu's Harriers, which was one of the last pairs of its kind to breed in Suffolk. We took turns to sit at a safe distance in order to prevent egg collectors from disturbing the nest. Sadly, 1967 was the last season they bred, but they were replaced by a pair of Marsh Harriers which were almost as rare in those days.

Dick persuaded me to join the STNC and I tried to do so. However, I managed to join something called the Suffolk Naturalists' Society which I later discovered was not the same organisation. I did eventually join the STNC, but more of that later.

Now I was at enjoying my obsession with birds much more thanks to my BTO role and with Minsmere and Carlton Marshes keeping me busy. A further big change in my life was just round the corner.

4.

Breeding Success

Our son Jeremy was born in 1969 and our daughter Bronwen followed a couple of years later. Now I had some real responsibilities. By now my attempts to be a pop star had come to an end and so more time could be spent thinking of birds.

In 1972 Cliff Waller came to Suffolk to be warden of the Walberswick National Nature Reserve. I was already a regular at Walberswick and had been part of the Dingle Bird Club which studied the birds of the area, including carrying out activities such as ringing. I first met Cliff in The Plough Inn at Wangford, and this was the beginning of a long friendship which endures to this day. Cliff had previously worked as a warden on Fair Isle, Shetland, and Lundy, Devon, and his tales of great rarities began to excite me and other birders in Suffolk. At that time Cliff had a considerable influence on my birding life and he too had some interesting approaches to wetland habitat creation and conservation.

It was not long before Cliff was encouraging us to accompany him all around the UK in search of rare birds. Yes, we were twitching. I saw so many birds with Cliff and others, and made so many long journeys which were daft in retrospect. Once a group of us drove up to Hartlepool, arriving at dawn to see a White-billed Diver, then we travelled across to north Wales for a Cattle Egret. Reflecting on the thousands of Cattle Egrets I have now seen around the world since, it does seem a bit stupid. That was far from an isolated long-haul trip, though. Once we headed down to Exeter for a Hudsonian Godwit and then up to Gwent for an American Bittern. Other times we dashed down to Cornwall for Belted Kingfisher, Kent for Great Bustard, Hampshire for Scops Owl, and so on and so on. Cliff also demonstrated how it was possible to get to Cambridgeshire at first light, see a Sociable Lapwing and then get back to Suffolk and be in my office in Beccles by 9am. Crazy stuff!

At this time Cliff also encouraged some of us to make the annual October pilgrimage to the Isles of Scilly. Participants included Brian Brown, Tony Butcher, George Maybury and various others. This was an amazing time in my birding life. I managed to visit for nine consecutive years, seeing a lot of very rare birds in the process and also meeting a lot of friendly birders from around the UK. Many of them, and in particular Peter Basterfield, are still pals today. The islands had an unreal quality about them, and it was here that I got to know the late David Hunt who met a grisly end with a Tiger in Corbett National Park in India. There was little technology on the islands in those days so you actually needed to talk to people to find out what was about. It was dangerous to stay indoors because you might not be aware of what birds were being found. You had to get up, get out and find out the news.

Myself and others once jogged after a chap clad in a Barbour jacket, and on catching him asked him what he was going after. We were a bit shocked and embarrassed to find out that he was not a birder at all, but he was just late for his lunch. On another memorable occasion a large crowd of birders had gathered on St Mary's Airfield in the evening in the hope of seeing an American Nighthawk which had been found there the previous night. Right on cue this American nightjar emerged and put on a spectacular show before disappearing as the gloom gathered. Then the most extraordinary thing happened. The throng of birders got to their feet and there followed a spontaneous round of applause just as if they had been an appreciative audience at a concert.

Another of the great characters of Scilly in those days was Mike Rogers. Mike was a chain-smoking ex-police officer who was also Secretary to the British Birds Rarities Committee. One morning we bumped into Mike standing puffing away by a thick hedge. He beckoned us over explaining that the gentle 'check check' noise we could hear coming from the thicket might be a Melodious Warbler. Bowing to his great experience we stayed with him for at least 30 minutes. We peered into the hedge and strained our ears at this constant and rhythmic 'check check'.

Boredom and cigarette smoke finally got the better of us and we moved on. We turned a corner so we were on the other side of the hedge and the noise we had been hearing got a little louder. A bit further on we burst into laughter at the sight of a man cutting a massive hedge. His shears went 'check check' every time he cut. It shows how close all birders get to letting their obsession in the hunt for more species affect their brains. Poor old Mike was not convinced when we gave him the news that night.

There were so many super birds on these visits. I recall a Pallas's Warbler sitting in the same bush as a Scarlet Tanager and reflected that the East had really come face to face with the West. This was at a time when the Cold War was at its most tense. These large gatherings of birders did cause some incredible human behaviour. A Rose-breasted Grosbeak was rumoured to be present on The Garrison. Crowds gathered

Celebrating a sighting of Rose-breasted Grosbeak on the Isles of Scilly

and one excitable individual was convinced he could hear it calling. There was an avian noise which seemed to come from within the grounds of the Star Castle Hotel. Further investigation revealed that the noise was being made by a group of Budgerigars in an aviary.

Scilly is still a place that you can visit in autumn and see a lot of scarce migrants and vagrants of both Nearctic and Palearctic origin. I preferred the old days when there were almost no vehicles on the islands so you had to spend all day walking everywhere. The posh birders might have rented a bike and the more wealthy might have hired the odd taxi. But generally you just walked, trotted or ran flat out, depending on whether you had seen the species that you were heading to before. On recent visits walking the lanes has become a more hazardous occupation due to the volume of traffic on St Mary's.

I was delighted in later years to assist with the setting up of the Isles of Scilly Wildlife Trust. This enabled me to revisit the islands and also to take my wife to see where I had been running around after brightly coloured American birds for so many years.

It was not long after our Isles of Scilly exploits that I started to think that it might be better to travel more overseas to see birds in places where they actually belonged.

During this period my employer William Clowes had become part of a group called McCorquodale Books and I was invited by them to work at their headquarters based in Colchester. This would be quite an upheaval for the family as we had always lived close to our natal area. We made the important decision to move and set up home in the village of Boxted, just a few miles north of Colchester and on the southern slopes of the beautiful Stour Valley. It was to be our home for the next 24 years. Yes, I was now living just outside of my beloved Suffolk in north Essex.

Luckily I had relatives in the area as my mother came from Colchester. I also had a few birding contacts too. Simon and Pat Cox, the late Tony Marshall and Malcolm and Rosemary Wright all made it easy for me to settle down.

I discovered that our own village was pretty good for birds and the surrounding Stour Valley became one of my local patches. This included the tiny reservoir at Thorington Street. The other plus point was that I could still get to some of my favourite parts of the Suffolk coast in under an hour.

Tony Marshall made sure that I quickly discovered Abberton Reservoir, which is still a mecca for birders today, and I enjoyed many a good bird there over the years. It was here on the causeways that I also met many friendly and fine birders. I was surprised to discover just what a wonderful county Essex is for finding birds. A highlight in those days was to accompany Tony on one of his drives around the reservoir on the concrete edge. Nobody had told me that there was a stretch with a sloping camber and Tony's joy was to slip over the side at great speed and accelerate round until it stopped. The unsuspecting passenger was always on the waterside and I can assure you it was terrifying. When health and safety issues became topical this practise was probably very wisely banned.

For me Tony represented everything that birding at Abberton was about. He spent many hours there counting birds and, if there was not much about, studying the Mute Swans. He named each pair according to their temperament. One was Bert and Joan because they were dominant and belligerent, another Kerry and Audrey because they were sadly childless. The third pair was, he said, Derek and Beryl,

My dear friend Tony Marshall watching birds at his beloved Abberton Reservoir

who were trying so hard to breed but were young birds and lacking experience. He had a wicked sense of humour. When we were all on the Isles of Scilly Tony would often send my wife Beryl a postcard. I remember one in particular which said "Today I saw your husband desperately chasing a brightly coloured American bird. I thought you ought to know". Then he signed it "An Admirer." Tony also loved counting birds, indeed it was something of an obsession with him. He always used to tell me that two birds of the same species is a pair but three upwards is a flock. When he was on Scilly and I had returned home he would send me a postcard. On one occasion he reckoned the birds were so poor he had taken to counting dog breeds and was on 17. He was still looking hard for a Pomeranian, one of which he had been informed had been reported from Telegraph Hill on St Mary's.

I also recall seeing him in a queue in the Post Office on St Mary's. He had a huge smile on his face and looked very excited, informing everyone in the building that it was his first day for receiving the State pension and was it not truly wonderful that the Queen was now paying for him to go birding. To some it was a bit rich because Tony obviously had considerable private means since nobody in living memory ever knew him to have a job of any sort.

Tony was also a creature of habit. One morning I met him leaving Guntons, a well-known Colchester coffee shop.

Red-rumped Swallow – a species that caused obsessive behaviour in one of my friends

I asked him what birds he had seen and once again he complained of how few there were about. He shook me rigid by telling me that in his boredom he had begun counting "fat ladies" and had reached 18 that morning. His sense of humour lasted all of his life. Just prior to having to go into a nursing home where he sadly died I called and we started chatting. Suddenly I heard a knock on his door and he said "I shall have to go, the lady has come round to see if I am dead." What a character – there will never be another one like Tony.

I also got to know other Essex birders, including Peter Newton from Clacton, and between them all they made sure I saw plenty of birds. I also became more aware that my level of obsession was shared by others. I was standing at Abberton one evening watching, with many others, my first Red-rumped Swallow. Suddenly Peter was by my side frantically trying to get onto the bird. He was quickly satisfied but his agitation did not subside. I asked him what the problem was. "It's my wife Julie – she's in labour." "Is she in hospital?" I enquired. "No," he replied, "She's sitting in the car over there and I have told her to press the hooter hard if things get worse." I am pleased to report that all went smoothly with the birth and their son Simon turned out reasonably well. You see, birders at times appear to get their priorities a bit muddled.

It was during this period that I first met Major Bill Payn. Bill was the county bird recorder for Suffolk and lived at Hartest, not far from our new home. I had corresponded with Bill for some time and soon I began to pay him regular visits. He had of course written the latest county avifauna, *The Birds of Suffolk*, and was working on a second edition. In 1977 he had decided to give up the county recorder's job and suggested that I take it on. The Suffolk Bird Report formed part of the Transactions of the Suffolk Naturalists' Society in those days, but the growing number of Suffolk birders were calling for a stand-alone publication.

With a lot of support from newly found Ipswich friends like Steve Piotrowski and Philip Murphy I did manage to pull that off, but not without causing some

Former Suffolk bird recorder Major William Payn skinning a Little Bittern in Spain

bad feeling between me and stalwarts of SNS. The latter was fully financing the report but was made up mainly of botanists, entomologists and the like and could not see why ornithologists should be treated differently. The outcome was the strengthening of the Suffolk Ornithologists' Group, which was formed in 1973, and the deveopment of a joint relationship which continues today.

Being county recorder and part of a new records committee threw up many challenges. I was also editing and producing the new bird report. I had immense support and assistance in those days from Philip Murphy, who loved statistics and historical records far more than me. We therefore seemed to work well together. In those days we had no computers and all the records received were on paper. Also very few photographs were received. We worked long hours, meeting up on winter evenings to get the job done. We then packed up the original data and handed it over to the Suffolk Biological Records Centre in Ipswich Museum. The latter was a major step forward as previously dear old Bill Payn used to burn all the original records at the end of the year. It was so different to what happens today.

The proper rigidity of assessing records drew out the character of many an observer. One notorious local would see a national rarity most weeks but never submit a proper description of any of the birds. All we ever got was colourful words on the weather, habitat and such, but nothing about the bird. Needless to say he finally took up dragonfly recording. Another well-known birder took such complete umbrage at me and others judging his records that he declared his dislike of me and avoided ever meeting me.

Even normally sensible birders can get most unreasonable if they are not able to see rare birds, which they consider is their right. In 1984 another well-known birder called me to say that a local farmer at Pettistree had heard a strange bird song and had seen the bird in question delivering it. He did not want any twitchers on the farm but would appreciate some help with the identification. We went along and discovered what is still Suffolk's only River Warbler. When this record was published a while later there was uproar from some birders because they had not been allowed to see the bird. I found all of this extraordinary but persevered with the recording task.

It is probably worth reflecting on a few other controversial birding incidents in Suffolk. In 1982 Mike Marsh discovered a small 'peep' on the shingle at Felixstowe Ferry. His initial identification was that the bird was a Western Sandpiper – a North American species which is extremely rare in the UK. He came to that conclusion because of its longish bill in comparison to the slightly commoner, but still very rare, Semipalmated Sandpiper. The Landguard ringers made a few attempts to catch the bird but failed, so there was an element of doubt surrounding the identification. The bird was most co-operative, though, staying from October until the following April. This was in the days before high quality photo equipment was widely available, so not many good pictures were taken.

The outcome was that hundreds of birders saw the bird and some were suggesting it was in fact Semipalmated Sandpiper. And after papers were published it was indeed accepted as that species. What is controversial is that the original observer was never contacted by the Rarities Committee and the late Peter Grant, the great Guru of rare birds and Chairman of that body, never came to see the bird. In the event, the whole saga gave lots of birders something to talk about.

Another controversy of bird recording in East Anglia is that our neighbours in Norfolk stubbornly refuse to stick to the Watsonian boundaries generally agreed as the preferred borders. This gives consistency to recording areas and takes no notice of any subsequent boundary changes. A wonderful example of the outcome of such nonsense was a Killdeer seen on the south side of Breydon Water in 2006 and reported in the bird reports of both counties as first for the county. Same bird in the same field on the same dates.

We also had a couple of birds in Suffolk that caused a lot of discussion and speculation. In February 1981 a coot at Alton Water showed some features that suggested to some observers that this bird might be an American Coot. One of the latter had just been seen in Ireland and some Suffolk birders had been over to see it. This bird led birders a merry dance right through to the spring of 1982. We called the bird a 'Moot' all along because we had suspicions that it might be a hybrid between a Common Moorhen and a Eurasian Coot. Eventually we did find examples of where this had happened and another bird in Yorkshire was somewhat similar and was conveniently referred to as a 'Coohen'. Our bird was a bit smaller than a Eurasian Coot, had a very indistinct colour to the frontal shield, lobed feet and behaved like a Coot in the water, but was more like a Common Moorhen when on land.

In April 1982 Trevor Charlton found an unusual Yellowhammer in a field at Sizewell. The bird was superficially like a male Yellowhammer, but with less yellow on the face and this being replaced by white and a tinge of chestnut. Indeed the bird became known as the Sizewell Bunting and some even suggested *Emberiza nucleari* as a suitable scientific name. It was some years before the mystery was solved. It seems that where Yellowhammers and Pine Buntings breed close together hybrids can occur. A Russian scientist, on seeing the one poor photograph taken of the Sizewell bird, confirmed that it did indeed resemble a Yellowhammer x Pine Bunting hybrid. Half a tick then?

Away from birds my life was beginning to get difficult. After moving my family to Colchester my employer, McCorquodale Books, had a change of heart about centralising operations in the town and I found myself made redundant as I steadfastly refused to relocate to Liverpool. I managed to find a new job quickly at Tiptree Book Services in Tiptree itself, and although a more minor post it rescued the situation for the immediate future. It was also close enough to Abberton Reservoir for me to enjoy a lunchtime sandwich there. One such trip resulted in me finding a White-winged Tern one autumn. I might have regularly been a bit late back to the office in the afternoons in those days.

After three years I moved on to work for Seawheel, a shipping company based in Ipswich. Much of my work involved some travel to Belgium, The Netherlands, France and Germany. This immediately gave me an opportunity to do some foreign birding, at least in the summer months. I know I used to disappoint local staff who wanted to take me out on the town, but I much preferred to be in local woods searching for Black Woodpeckers, Short-toed Treecreepers and Crested Tits.

Back in the early 1970s I had met David Tomlinson at Minsmere on a golden day when a female Wilson's Phalarope was feeding on the scrape. It was a day when the reserve had been closed to the public and David Mower, the assistant warden, had found David wandering down the beach and had brought him in to see this North American jewel. When Herbert Axell turned up he evicted David on the grounds of him working for the *Shooting Times*, which was considered a heinous crime by the great man. This did not hinder a friendship developing between David and myself and when a few years later he and others started up bird racing as a form of fund raising for wildlife I responded to his requests for help.

Over the next year or so Steve Piotrowksi and I provided a 'back-up team' for David's Country Life team, which was so named because by that time he had become Assistant Editor of that magazine. The 'official team' consisted of David, the then Minsmere Warden Jeremy Sorenson, local boy and original bird racer Peter Smith and school teacher Bill Urwin. The idea was that we would find and stake out all the birds needed throughout East Anglia. David and I

The author (right) with the very successful Country Life bird race team

were both very competitive and could not consider for one
moment being beaten by the Flora & Fauna Preservation
Society team of John Gooders, TV Goodie Bill Oddie,
Tim Inskipp from CITES and my old mate Cliff Waller.
John Gooders was extremely well known having written a
series of *Where to Watch Birds ...* books. He was a lovable
reprobate who smoked and drank more than was good for
him and was a real character who ended up being the Mayor
of Winchelsea in Sussex shortly before his death. I visited
his grave recently and thought he would be impressed that
comedian Spike Milligan is buried just a few feet away. Both
men were equally entertaining.

We treated the events like a military operation, using

The author with fellow bird race back-up man Steve Piotrowski

all our good knowledge and birding friends, and never ever
came second. Channel 4 produced a film of the event in
1982 and the next year Collins published a book on the
event written by David, John and Bill Oddie. The most
important outcome, though, was we raised thousands of
pounds for nature conservation projects.

Later we challenged *Dutch Birding* to a similar event.
A team including David again, Peter Smith, Bill Urwin
and Bill Oddie went over to The Netherlands whilst the
Dutch came over to UK. Once again Steve Piotrowski and I
provided a back-up service and accompanied the team to The
Netherlands. It was more difficult in a country where we had
to start from scratch, but true to form we soundly beat our

European neighbours. However, to my personal annoyance they got a Ross's Gull in Norfolk, which is a species that I have still never seen.

At this time several observers were coming to the conclusion that Landguard Point was a very important site for migrant birds and warranted further study. Areas of scrub close to Felixstowe Docks were regularly turning up very good birds indeed. Perhaps the most spectacular find was a Lark Sparrow, a vagrant from North America, found by Trevor and Lesley Charlton as they botanised on Landguard Common on 30th June 1981. I remember getting a call in my office in Ipswich asking me to come as soon as possible and to bring an American field guide as they were confident they had a 'stonker'. It was the first record of this species in the UK but was not accepted as a wild bird until another turned up at Winterton, Norfolk, on 15th May 1991.

Richard Woolnough, Conservation Officer for the Suffolk Trust for Nature Conservation which ran the reserve, encouraged a few of us to try and set up a bird observatory on the site. With permission from English Heritage, the owners of the fenced off area of scrub and the old military buildings, a few of us sat down to discuss the possibility. In the old seawatching hide, and by the light of a Tilley Lamp, Richard, Steve Piotrowski, Mick Wright, Bill Last and I had the first meeting and we decided to give it a go with me as founding chairman.

The author bird ringing with Philip Murton at Landguard Point

The first task was to get the buildings into some sort of order, so work days were held and after a while we had a ringing room, office and so on. There was a problem with ringing, though. I was the only one with any ringing experience, but I held only a C Permit. We managed to persuade Philip Murton to join us. He had until recently worked for the Essex Trust for Nature Conservation and his skills were essential since he had an A Permit and was a licenced trainer. Perhaps more importantly he brought with him Dick Hipkin, who turned out to be a key person in setting up Landguard Bird Observatory.

Philip was not a big player with respect to Landguard, but Dick turned out to be the backbone in those early days, lifting us all up when we struggled and turning his hand to anything to ensure we succeeded. Perhaps the biggest task was constructing an enormous Heligoland trap behind the buildings which once caught an Arctic Skua. Sadly Dick did not live long enough to fully enjoy Landguard after the formative days of the observatory. Soon others came to join in – Rex Beecroft, another trainer, and fledgling ringers Reg Clarke, Mike Marsh and Roger Beecroft. The Observatory was officially opened by Herbert Axell in 1983 and quickly gained strength. It continues today as an independent charity, adding significantly to the ornithological knowledge of Suffolk.

There have been some extraordinary birds found at Landguard and those who predicted its potential as a site for migrants and vagrants deserve much credit. Over the years I came face to face with Blyth's Pipit, Pied and Desert Wheatears, Yellow-billed Cuckoo, Thrush Nightingale, Red-flanked Bluetail, Spectacled, Dusky and Radde's Warblers and many more rare and scarce species. This remarkable record continues and extraordinary species like Trumpeter Finch and Short-toed Treecreeper have followed, although I am told that the numbers of birds have declined a little.

The explanation for the site's attractiveness to migrants has been discussed at length. The reason, in addition to its geographical location, may be the massive Felixstowe Docks, which are situated adjacent to the reserve. It has been well documented that nocturnal migrating birds navigate using the stars, and if these are obliterated by rain or cloud then the birds will 'fall'. That is they will land, and when this happens they are often attracted by powerful lights. The lights at Felixstowe Docks were immensely powerful. In fact once, when I was on the now defunct Zeebrugge to Felixstowe ferry, the captain demonstrated to us that the glow from Felixstowe could be seen from nearly 40 nautical miles out. Any bird high up in the sky could see it from much further away. Thus we assumed that we got so many migrants because of the attraction of these lights.

Landguard Bird Observatory also ringed birds in the shelter belts planted when the Dock was extended. Once again many more birds than expected were caught, including rarities like Blyth's Reed Warbler and Arctic Warbler. Then one day John Gummer, the then Secretary of State for the Environment, quite properly chided the Dock management for not using more eco-friendly bulbs. They promptly changed the bulbs and the effect was immediate and no longer did the unusually high numbers of migrants turn up in the area.

This effect was noticed elsewhere. Lowestoft had always been a haven for rarities, but Brian Brown pointed out that in his opinion finding migrants and rarities in Lowestoft became more difficult during Landguard's heyday. He concluded that the 'Felixstowe Glow' sucked all the good

The author with Herbert Axell and others at the opening of Landguard Bird Observatory

stuff down to Landguard. Certainly a good number of rarities have been found in Lowestoft again since the changes at Felixstowe. This theory is totally without any science to support it but nevertheless fun to consider.

As the years went by Landguard also stimulated an interest in ringing birds and studying their migration in my son Jeremy. He became so enthusiastic and quickly very competent. It was the science involved in the work which really got him hooked. Because of this great bonus in my life we set up ringing stations nearer home. We had a site in scrub woodland next to the reservoir at Thorington Street, we ringed winter thrushes in the orchards in Boxted and also, with the help and support of Edward Jackson, set up

Edward Jackson and the author emptying a mist net at Flatford Mill

activities at Flatford Mill. Flatford was a wonderful place and also with the help of friend John Turner we had many happy and productive sessions there.

Jeremy progressed to a 'C' permit, which meant that he could catch and ring birds on his own. I would often come home to find that he had caught a species in our garden which I had never seen there. Sadly when he left university and started working abroad he discovered that bird ringing was only allowed if you were a professional ornithologist, so his activity in this respect waned considerably.

By now I was also trying to encourage more people to develop their latent interest in birds by travelling around the county giving courses on identification and other skills under the auspices of the Workers' Educational Association or Cambridge Extramural Studies. I remember my first effort very well, and it took place in the Suffolk village of Chelmondiston, close to the picturesque Pin Mill on the River Orwell. It gladdens me to know that many of the people who attended that course are now experienced birders who contribute much to Suffolk ornithology. Many others who I met through these events also took up birding seriously and enhance the growing numbers of people caring about Suffolk's birds.

5.

Conservation Beckons

During the early 1980s my career in industry began to stumble quite a bit, but soon there came an opportunity which was to change my life and that of my family very considerably indeed.

In the autumn of 1984 I was approached again by Richard Woolnough, who suggested that I should apply for the new post of Director of the Suffolk Trust for Nature Conservation. This was, ironically, the organisation I had once tried to join as a member but without a great deal of success. However, I was now a member and a volunteer member of the Conservation Committee. I consulted my family over Sunday lunch and will never forget the response

The family looking for Honey Buzzards at Felbrigg Hall in the 1970s

of my daughter Bronwen, who was then aged about 13. "Oh Daddy you should go for it, and anyway we won't need you in a year or two's time". Well I am glad to say the Bronwen still needs me.

I also received enormous support and encouragement from John O'Sullivan, who was the Regional Officer for the RSPB in Norwich. We had become good friends and he knew I was quite keen to break into the nature conservation field. He convinced me that I could do the job and what is more that I would really enjoy the challenge.

There was a lot to consider, especially as the children were not yet through secondary school and we hoped that university years beckoned. We coped and eventually Jeremy went off to Cambridge where he achieved a degree in Natural Sciences and Bronwen to Oxford Brookes University where she achieved a degree in Hotel Management and Catering. We were delighted as they were the first children on either side of our family to attend university at all.

The other consideration was that if I was successful then I would take a big drop in salary, but my wonderful wife Beryl suggested that she could get a job and our income would not be too badly affected. I applied for the job at the last minute and was invited for an interview. I was already quite well known to the panel, especially to Howard Mendel who then worked at the Ipswich Museum. After the interview I heard nothing for some time until they asked me to attend a

Saturday meeting with the full Council when I and another candidate would be considered by them.

I did not like the sound of this process and told the then Chairman George Lockett that I wanted no part of such a charade and that I would consider withdrawing my application. A couple of weeks later I was at a Suffolk Naturalists' Society meeting, of which I was Chairman, when Howard Mendel walked in and offered his congratulations. He immediately noticed my look of shock and asked if I had been contacted. I had not, but apparently it had been agreed that I would be offered the job.

I accepted of course, but that process was par for the course in terms of the amateurish way in which such organisations were run in those days. This became even more apparent when I started my dream job in nature conservation on 1st January 1985.

It came as a huge shock on arriving at the Trust's office in Saxmundham to find Colonel Tom Pares, the General Secretary and the previous head of staff at the Trust, still in residence. The Council had employed me but not yet found a way of telling him that I was taking over. He had been told that his services were no longer required but had decided to stay on to tidy up loose ends This was entirely unsatisfactory from my point of view and it took some effort to arrange his exit so that I could get started.

I had always had a good relationship with Conservation

Officer Richard Woolnough and admired what he had done in raising the profile and activity of the Trust. Sadly it was obvious after a few weeks in the post that our working relationship was to deteriorate rapidly. Richard was used to doing his own thing and responded in a negative way to my plans for applying some basic management ethics as simple as filling in a timesheet. He also suggested that he should not report to me as his line manager, but instead to the Chairman. This was intolerable to me and he did not get his way. Richard had a good reputation for motivating and getting people working for wildlife, but seemed to detest any sense of order. It was a relief for both of us when he announced that he was taking up a post at the then Royal Society for Nature Conservation. Having said that I still admire what Richard did for the Trust, and without him I would have had little to work on. At a later date he was also tremendously supportive as a Trustee with my efforts to get a permanent headquarters for the Trust.

Now it was time to get down to business. The Trust only employed about five staff and more than 200 were recruited through the government's Manpower Services Commission scheme. These were basically unemployed people who worked in habitat teams carrying out conservation work throughout the county. I was very unhappy upon arrival to discover that the scheme was run from outside the Trust, and by an individual who cared little for nature conservation.

I did eventually manage to integrate the scheme and Mark Rose was appointed to run that part of the operation. With his involvement things improved greatly.

By now I had made a major discovery. These conservation people did not all like birds. This was a major blow. All they talked about was botany and something called habitats. I had so much to learn. I was lucky that another Beccles boy, Peter Lawson, already worked for the Trust and he quickly introduced me to the joys of wild plants and the habitats of Suffolk. I might have weakened and given up in those early days of chaos without dear Peter. In addition my then Chairman, Peter Wilson, gave me a guide to identifying orchids with the inscription "To help you know what you are treading on when you are looking up." It was donated and received with considerable humour.

I found that the staff did have a good sense of humour. Towards the end of my first summer as Director we issued a press release to celebrate the blooming of hundreds of Meadow Saffron on our Martin's Meadows reserve at Monewden. The press turned up and I was photographed admiring these superb flowers. What the staff had forgotten to tell me was the local Suffolk name for these plants. I suffered quite a bit of leg-pulling when my photograph appeared in the *East Anglian Daily Times* with the headline 'Trust Director in field with Naked Ladies'.

My confusion regarding the terminology and politics of

The author with Sir David Attenborough in Bradfield Woods, Suffolk, in 1984

nature conservation made the early days difficult. Everybody seemed to talk in acronyms so I concentrated on bringing some business discipline into the Trust. The staff was diligent and devoted, but many had little experience of working in a business office. It was a blow to discover that the perceived membership was much lower than estimated because many people were no longer paying their membership fees and others had never upgraded their subscriptions from the original £1. There were no computers in those days and everything was done manually.

The other challenge was to learn how to work with a mixture of wonderful volunteers and paid staff. The former were highly motivated and everything they did was with the best of intentions. A challenge was to get staff to see how much volunteers could contribute in exchange for patience and training.

Just as I immersed myself in office detail there came a chance to stand up and fight for my beloved birds. The Felixstowe Dock and Railway Company announced that they were seeking permission to remove more than 400 acres of inter-tidal mudflats on the River Orwell in order to extend their quay space. The river was a Site of Special Scientific Interest (SSSI) but we knew that Government could override this designation in favour of the 'National Need'. This was during the prime ministership of Margaret Thatcher so we were not optimistic of a positive outcome. Felixstowe Dock did not have a Dock Union Scheme, so we could see that pushing for development there would be desirable to politicians.

The Trust joined together in partnership with the RSPB and Suffolk Ornithologists' Group and formed a campaign called OUT – Orwell Under Threat. This was a major undertaking for the Trust and I had to don my suits again and spend most of my time commuting between Suffolk and Westminster. This was the first time that opposition to a major development had been considered and it did the Trust no harm at all. Membership began to increase and the profile was raised by almost daily appearances on local Radio, TV and press.

As part of this effort I joined groups of wonderful volunteers led by Mick Wright (later to become warden of the new Trimley Marshes Nature Reserve) out on the freezing saltings at night catching and marking waders such as Common Redshank in order to monitor their movements throughout the estuary. We were indebted in those days to Dr Mike Moser, then working for the BTO, who supervised and encouraged us throughout these sessions. Regular high tide roost counts were also carried out at weekends, again using volunteers, to ensure that sufficient data was available to put our case to Parliament.

Trying to explain to industrialists and politicians the intricate relationship and dependency between wading birds and wildfowl and what to them was an expanse of smelly mud was a real challenge. Of course we did not win but we did not entirely lose either. The outcome was the designation of a new nature reserve – Trimley Marshes – adjacent to the new development and the finance to create that reserve and manage it for the next 35 years. Furthermore the partnership had prolonged the opposition for three years – much longer than Parliament or the Dock Company expected – and also forced them to spend considerably more money than budgeted. There was now a cost to destroying acres of valuable habitat.

The land on which the new dock extension was to be built, and indeed the land for the nature reserve, are owned by Trinity College, Cambridge, and the ends that they went too to ensure the development took place were amazing. A new community centre for Trimley village ensured the support of locals. That gave me even greater stimulus to continue our fight.

Our involvement in this matter gave the Trust significant presence in Suffolk thereafter. We had arrived and were regarded as an organisation which stood up for the environment and did so in a thoroughly professional manner. We never looked back and began to build the organisation from that base. This was my first taste of such a scrap and not only did I find it exhilarating, but it gave me great confidence that I could achieve something in the world of nature conservation.

The final chapter in this tale happened when the Felixstowe Dock and Railway Company threw a pretentious and extravagant opening for their new extension. I was invited and just before the event kicked off I was extolling my regrets at losing our precious mudflats to Kim Riley, the BBC *Look East* Chief Reporter. I was a bit taken aback when he asked me to repeat my words to camera. I should not have been surprised when that evening the BBC local news headlined the dock opening but started off with my piece saying that this was a bleak day for our wildlife. The next day the people at the Dock Company were furious because we had stolen a little bit of their thunder. Just another reminder that the Suffolk Wildlife Trust had arrived.

As a result of the permission to create the Dock extension being granted, the Suffolk Wildlife Trust began the construction of Trimley Marshes Nature Reserve. Money was allocated by the Dock Company for its creation and management. Roger Beecroft was appointed as Project Officer and very soon work began. We had learned a bit about wetland recreation from my previous experiences at Minsmere and we had also researched several created wetlands in other parts of Europe. We discovered that if you impound water permanently the food content for birds declines over time. We decided therefore create two large areas, one which would be flooded in summer and the other in winter. A third area contains permanent water and

Trimley Marshes Nature Reserve – created after the Felixstowe Dock & Railway Bill

therefore always has birds. This was constructed to appease the birders.

When the reserve was completed we had become tenants of Trinity College. During the debate over the Dock extension I had once met Dr John Bradfield, the Bursar of the college. He contacted me one day to ask about the location of rare orchid species which occurred in Suffolk. Despite us having differing opinions about the Dock I offered to get somebody to show him the orchids and also gave him a copy of *The Orchids of Suffolk* by Martin Sandford. Much later I was surprised to I received an invitation from the college to an Occasional Tenants' Dinner to celebrate the retirement of the Bursar.

This was an exceptionally grand affair with several hundred guests all in full evening dress. When my wife and I arrived we could not find our names anywhere on the vast seating plan. We began to wonder if we were at the right event. Presently a young chap from the land agency Bidwells appeared and whisked off Beryl as she was to be his guest. He then indicated to me that I was Dr Bradfield's guest and was seated on the top table with the master, a couple of dons and the Bursar. This was heady company for a Grammar School failure and was most unexpected. My nerves did not improve when I was passed the port in a silver jug presented to the college by none other than Henry VIII. I was even more staggered when John Bradfield mentioned me at length in his speech. He was apparently impressed that we could have been at loggerheads in the dock debate but I still took the trouble to arrange for him to be shown the rare orchids.

It was in 1987 that I agreed with Chris Durdin of the RSPB in Norwich that SWT would join in organising an event to publicise its 'Stop the Massacre' campaign, which was drawing attention to the wholesale slaughter of migrant birds in the Mediterranean countries. The event was held at the aptly named Sparrow's Nest Theatre in Lowestoft. Bill Oddie agreed to be one of the speakers along with other birders like Bryan Bland who are well known in East Anglia. It was an astonishing event and amazing that we could fill a theatre with a number of people standing on a stage with no

The author and Chris Durdin receiving the Eyewatch Award from Prince Charles

pictures or other aids describing the horrors of bird killing seen on their travels.

One of the outcomes was that we received an Eyewatch Award, partly because it was the European Year of the Environment and also mainly thanks to Chris's efforts. The award was presented to Chris and I in London by the Prince of Wales. It was to be the first of many awards won by SWT.

Even more inspiring was that a young girl, probably aged about 12 or 13, called Nathalie Seddon also received an award that evening. She had persuaded her parents to buy a woodland in her home village and she had set it up as a community woodland involving local people as volunteers. She was a most confident and resourceful young person and hearing her story and meeting her gave me tremendous inspiration and great hope for the youth of our country. It is somewhat heartening to know that she is now Dr Nathalie Seddon, a Research Fellow at Oxford University in the Department of Zoology.

One of the annual events of the year for the Trust was The Suffolk Show. We once had a small presence there, which at the time was like thrusting Daniel into the lions' den. In my first year, 1985, an article had appeared in the Trust's magazine slamming the efforts of west Suffolk farmers in planting trees and hedges. The Stanton Survey as it was called surveyed 50 square miles of farmland, discovering 380 miles of hedgerows and 543 ponds. The study was conducted

David Barker, John Cousins and Juliet Hawkins – positive campaigners for wildlife on the farm in jocular mood

to illustrate that some farmers really did care about the countryside. The magazine article reduced the significance of the findings, being critical of the destruction of these features in Suffolk.

The outcome was that at the Suffolk Show that year I was confronted by a very angry farmer dressed in a suit and a bowler hat who I later discovered was David Barker, the author of the survey. David was County NFU Chairman at that time and I was able to calm him and offer him equal space in the next magazine to get his point of view across.

David and I became lifelong friends after this event and it was he who made me realise that the trust needed to engage with the farming fraternity if wildlife was to have any chance in what was largely an agricultural county. The Farming and Wildlife Advisory Group (FWAG) had just been set up, and it was joining in with that effort which enabled the first step to be made. The impressive Juliet Hawkins was the first professional advisor and was making huge efforts to get farmers involved, and being part of the team at FWAG was a major opportunity for the Trust to help and make new friends. Indeed it was not long before David Barker and another enthusiastic farmer, John Cousins, had persuaded the Suffolk Agricultural Association to set aside a space in order to construct a wildlife area on the Suffolk showground where the Trust, FWAG and others would be based on show days. The association became very proud of that area and ensured that all important visitors went and had a look. This helped a great deal in raising the profile of the work being done jointly between farmers and conservationists, and brought more people to the table.

This partnership thrived and at the time when John Gummer was Minister of Agriculture he encouraged a delegation of us to go to Brussels and lobby for the introduction of set-aside to do something positive for wildlife. Previously it was seen only as a food reduction policy to help alleviate surpluses such as the much talked about 'grain mountains'. The trouble was that nobody had considered how farmers would manage that land and as it turned out fields of set-aside were being cut at the peak time for nesting birds. I was publicly very negative about set-aside and it was Suffolk farmer John Cousins who took me to task and explained how effective it might be. He too was part of that delegation.

Our plea was that the 10 per cent of land that farmers had to take out of production could be enhanced for wildlife by creating permanent features on field margins and unproductive land. The thing that shook the politicians most was that farmers and conservationists were coming hand in hand to ask for the same thing. The outcome was that permanent set-aside prescriptions were allowed, with more sensible management of the annual areas as well.

Just after that John Gummer appointed me as the first nature conservationist to sit on a Regional Agriculture Advisory Panel. This enabled me to continue to encourage the farming community to work with conservationists on future issues in the countryside. It was also at this time that John Cousins came up with the idea of "Green Veins through the Countryside". This progressed to a BBC2 documentary in which I took part, along with John and Juliet Hawkins, to try and illustrate not only how important it was to link up existing natural features but also to enhance them by using this permanent set-aside. This would allow more important and other permanent features to be covered by agri-environment schemes. This seemed to work well and whilst

The Duke of Gloucester presenting the author with an award from The Suffolk Agricultural Association

set-aside was running it gave wildlife a new chance in the modern farmed environment. More importantly it brought some of the farming community closer to some nature conservationists. I was therefore delighted to accept an award from the Suffolk Agricultural Society in 2006 in recognition of getting farmers and conservationists working together.

I am so delighted that all of David's family are now close friends and I am particularly delighted that oldest son Patrick and his cousin Brian are now running the farm with an even greater emphasis on nature conservation. They have been very successful and have won a number of national awards. It gives me hope that their generation will be able to break down the prejudices against wildlife which may have existed

The author with Patrick and Brian Barker at Westminster on the evening when they were presented with the Silver Lapwing Award

amongst the older farming fraternity. It gives me even greater pleasure that Patrick is a birder and bird ringer. I cannot think who gave him that idea.

There are many stories from those days, but I remember most the visit of Princess Margaret. Prior to her arrival at the wildlife area I was approached by Peggy Cole, who is something of a Suffolk celebrity. She played Mum in the acclaimed Ronald Blyth film *Akenfield*. Peggy also wrote a column on gardening and other things in the local paper and often appeared on local radio. She asked if I could introduce her to Princess Margaret as they were old friends. I pointed out that I was under strict instructions as to who she could meet and if I strayed from the programme I could be in trouble. I suggested she should stand by the marquee doorway and we would see what could be done. I have to confess that I did wonder if Peggy was getting a bit carried away with her local celeb status. However, as I was showing the royal visitor around and approaching the marquee she suddenly shouted out "Peggy" and headed straight over to her, much to the alarm of the security men. It seems that Peggy and the Princess did know each other rather well and used to spend time in Peggy's well-ordered council house drinking tea. Great days!

Over the years we also had visits to the wildlife area from the Duke of Edinburgh, Princess Anne, the Duke and Duchess of Kent, Princess Alexandra and the Duke and Duchess of Gloucester.

The Manpower Services Commission scheme eventually came to an end and the Trust took the very brave step of spending its cash reserve on employing the habitat supervisors and obtaining as many grants and as much sponsorship as possible in order to carry on growing the charity. The purchase of land for nature reserves was a great part of what I was doing in those days and we certainly added interesting sites such as Reydon Wood, Hen Reedbeds, Castle Marshes, Hazelwood Marshes, Lackford Lakes, Bonny Wood, Darsham Marshes, Spouse's Vale, Winks Meadow and Dingle Marshes. The acquisition of Castle Marshes at Barnby was a red letter day for me because these were some of the

Castle Marshes – my childhood haunt later purchased as a Suffolk Wildlife Trust reserve

marshes that I had trespassed on as a boy and now I could go there without trepidation. The owner was tickled pink when I told him he had just sold the land to that little old boy and his dog who he had chased off so many times. It was now apparent that owning additional land in turn led to a need for a strong staff structure to manage these important sites.

Buying land for nature reserves can lead to a maze of problems. The most straightforward cases are when everybody in the area is positive about the Trust being involved. One of the first reserves I helped to establish was Lackford Lakes. Bernard Tickner, a Trust supporter and the inventor of Abbot Ale, had already bought an option on some worked out gravel pits at Lackford and he wished to invoke this in favour of SWT. This was done and eventually, with Bernard's support, much more land was added and later some more and the visitor centre built. This took several phases and was in fact completed long after I had moved on.

Other acquisitions were more complex. Conservation staff had for some time identified Hazelwood Marshes near Aldeburgh as a prime wetland site which we should have on our wish list. Marsh Harrier, Avocet, Common Redshank, Northern Lapwing and Bearded Tit were all known to use the marshes and all of these species probably bred. The owner, Mark Partridge, had enjoyed a good relationship with the Trust for some time, so it was relatively simple to agree a price and start the proces. However, it did not turn out to be that easy.

Volunteer Rodney West took me to have tea with a group of people who lived in large houses overlooking the site. It was an agreeable experience and on the face of it nobody present seemed unhappy with us being the future owners. Indeed, two people offered to volunteer when the purchase was completed. Imagine my surprise later when I discovered that another bid had topped ours and it was alleged to have come from these same people. Well, Mark was not having it and we bought the reserve. The problems did not stop there, though.

The neighbouring Blackheath Estate also tried to get our purchase blocked by appealing to the 'County Set' to get us to back off. I am pleased to say that this did not work either. One of the adjoining householders became extremely objectionable. He trespassed regularly on our land to walk his dog, insisted a bird hide should have its roof lowered to improve his view (he lived on a hill at least 600 yards from the hide) and gatecrashed a meeting SWT was having with councillors to determine the problem.

One complaint I did receive via John Gummer did make a very valid point. A trader from Aldeburgh was concerned that having purchased an SSSI there would be nothing to stop us building a visitor centre and putting in a coffee shop and taking trade away from the town. We had no intention of doing any such thing but the point was well made.

We had a very strong support in those days from what was called the Nature Conservancy Council. It was always supportive in terms of grants and assistance with management. Part of this support was making Redgrave and Lopham Fen and Bradfield Woods into National Nature Reserves. This increased the resources which the Trust could channel into reserve management.

It was during this period that Jane Madgwick joined the staff and brought a huge degree of new thinking and energy to the Trust. She also quite liked birds. Jane, through contacts with the Countryside Commission, suggested that we should introduce an Open Reserves Policy to all our sites. This meant a funded programme of better signage and information, but most important of all open access for everyone whether or not they were members. This was extremely appealing to me and indeed the Trustees of the Trust and we pressed on with great zeal. We were therefore quite unprepared for the outbursts of protest from notable figures in the Wildlife Trust movement which followed. Their protestations of membership falling, damage to sites and so on never came to pass and our membership more than doubled. Most importantly we ceased to be seen as an elitist club and were not just concentrating our efforts on the converted. Soon most other Wildlife Trusts were following our example.

By this time it was obvious to many of us in Suffolk that the name Suffolk Trust for Nature Conservation was too long and unattractive. We felt that a more snappy and descriptive name would help the profile of the charity. With this in mind I proposed changing the name to Suffolk Wildlife Trust, complete with new symbolic logo. There was some heated opposition but I never understood the fears that 'Wildlife' did not include wild plants or that it only stood for lions, giraffes and the like.

My proposals were adopted and gradually all of the 47 Wildlife Trusts adopted similar titles, hence we now have a collective 'The Wildlife Trusts'. Rather sensibly the Royal Society for Nature Conservation (RSNC) also changed its name and became the Royal Society for Wildlife Trusts (RSWT).

The author receiving an Anglia Water award from the Queen Mother

From the early days I became more and more interested in the work of the collective 47 Wildlife Trusts. I had been warmly welcomed from the start by the first General Secretary, Franklyn Perring, and also by Tim Sands who worked for the RSNC/RSWT for years and who I used to meet regularly.

Many Trusts were in a transition period at this time, engaging more professional staff, although others were still run very much as local natural history societies. There was real tension between Trustees and the new breed of conservationists. Trustees ranged from enthusiastic naturalists to local pillars of society including landowners. Some with extreme views reckoned that some Great and Good were planted as trustees of Wildlife Trusts to ensure that they never became 'a problem' for what they considered progress. In addition, some Trustees moved on to become 'Directors' in the early days. This was often a serious mistake. Many of these people had an enormous passion for wildlife but no business experience at all and their organisations suffered until things moved on. Thinking back, though, this was probably an essential aspect of the Wildlife Trusts' evolution.

I got very involved in UK issues and enjoyed immensely the friendship of those kindred spirits from around the UK. Suffolk was amongst those leading the way in those days and, as already alluded to, introduced measures which today are considered normal by most of the Trusts. I met many of the Wildlife Trust greats, including the wonderful Ted Smith, Christopher Cadbury, John McMeeking, Harry Green and the formidable Helen Brotherton. These people and many more had played a significant part in establishing the Wildlife Trusts.

The Directors/Chief Executives of the Wildlife Trusts still hold an annual event known as 'Dircon'. This annual assembly is essential to such an organisation, being an opportunity for people to meet kindred spirits for a spot of bonding as well as discussing important issues in running our respective organisations. Dircon would be held in a different county each year so there were great opportunities to see how each area conducted their business. We deviated from this a couple of times and I was delighted to organise

Wildlife Trust Directors at their Dircon at Upper Teesdale

the first Dircon outside the UK, when we travelled to
The Netherlands.

Here we were able to discuss partnerships with European
NGOs, meet representatives of Dutch NGOs and, most
important of all, take people to visit the extraordinary
Oostvaardersplassen nature reserve. I know that exploration
here changed the thinking regarding reserve acquisition and
management for many. More of that amazing reserve later.

Gary Mantle later organised a similar Dircon in the
Czech Republic, where we were able to explore future
relationships with the emerging East European NGOs. I
know that this was a great eye-opener for many and others
were able to appreciate the huge areas of wildlife interest and
their value, but also the fast approaching threats of neglect as

more country people were being enticed to the big cities and indeed outside of their countries in search of better jobs.

The great frustration throughout my dealings with the centre was that successive well-meaning RSNC Trustees made some very questionable appointments. Trying to unite 47 separate charities under one banner is difficult enough, but you need people who fully understand the culture of the movement and who have genuine enthusiasm for nature conservation. A mixture of ego and misunderstanding meant that for many years there was an unhealthy tension between the 47 trusts and the centre. Maybe that is bound to happen whatever the personalities. Thank goodness that now we have Stephanie Hilborne as CEO of The Wildlife Trusts. Stephanie, having been Director of the Nottinghamshire Wildlife Trust, fully understands her role and I hope that she receives the support to grow The Wildlife Trusts' network to its full potential.

If you wanted to set up a country-wide conservation movement today you probably would not decide on the existing model with such a bottom-up form of management. It could be a bit like herding cats, but having said that many of the Trusts punch well above their weight and make an immense difference for wildlife locally. Sadly there is still a minority holding back what could be the most powerful voice for wildlife in the land. Another real problem is that, being different charities, Wildlife Trusts are effectively competing with each other.

One point well-made is that the wealthier Trusts tend to be in the wealthy and heavily populated south-east of England, where the most destruction has taken place. This obviously gives those greater resources than those in more remote areas of the UK, where there is still significant biodiversity. The latter tend to have smaller populations and therefore smaller memberships and less resources. The Wildlife Trusts movement has no mechanism for a more even spread of resources throughout the UK.

As the years rolled by Suffolk Wildlife Trust continued to develop and grow. We now had the Heritage Lottery Fund which enabled organisations like ours to be braver in our aspirations. All Wildlife Trusts received large sums in the form of cash grants to improve the habitat and access management of their reserves. This was largely due to the vision and hard work of Gary Mantle, the Director of the Wiltshire Wildlife Trust. His energy, along with the work of Andrew Davies, the Wildlife Trusts' Lottery Officer, meant that we were able to maximise opportunities.

That is not to say that finding funding was easy. Even HLF grants had to be matched with local funding. One of the problems was the amount of time taken to make decisions by the funders. This did at times lead to missed opportunities. The biggest problem is funding the core of the operation, and still no solution has been found to this problem.

There were also funding opportunities from Europe and we were successful in being awarded over £1 million by the LIFE fund to restore one of the most important reserves in Suffolk. Redgrave and Lopham Fen is partly situated in neighbouring Norfolk, at the head of the River Waveney. It was at this site that the meeting took place in 1961 where the decision to set up the Trust was taken. Essex & Suffolk Water, The Environment Agency and English Nature were essential partners in this mammoth effort to ensure that this important wetland was once again functioning properly.

The biggest problem was that the water company had installed a borehole adjoining the fen and years of abstraction had dried out the area significantly. Part of the plan was to site a new borehole further away from the reserve. The main task for reserve staff was to remove over 80 acres of scrub and trees which were also contributing to the drying out process. This was a difficult public relations task, mainly because in most peoples' lifetime the reserve had always been full of trees, and they might have grown to consider that situation to be appropriate. We issued press releases before starting work and that seemed to alleviate the concerns of most people. The reserve was reduced to a 'moonscape' first before once again becoming a wetland haven for wildlife.

We had a list of plants which had been present on the site during the 1950s, compiled as part of David Bellamy's PhD, and at least half of these returned fairly quickly. The most

Redgrave and Lopham Fen after wetland restoration work had taken place

important resident of the reserve was the Fen Raft Spider, since at that time this was its only known site in the UK. Evidence now suggests that this creature has held on but that its population has not increased. Thankfully populations of this remarkable species have since been discovered on the Pevensey Levels in Sussex and on the Swansea Canal in south Wales. In addition, thanks to hard work by Dr Helen Smith, Natural England and SWT, these rare and fascinating spiders have been introduced to new and suitable sites in East Anglia and appear to be thriving.

The recovery of the reserve also assisted other species as well. The areas of open water attracted many species of dragonflies and thereafter Eurasian Hobbies, which prey on them. This smart little falcon now breeds nearby. Also some of the plants noted by David Bellamy but thought to have been lost have been seen again around the Fen.

I have already mentioned that I had to get used to using local media in promoting the work of the Trust. First of all I owe much to David Green and John Grant, who were part of Eastern Counties Newspapers. David was the Environmental Correspondent for the *East Anglian Daily Times* and fellow birder John Grant was then working as a reporter in the Woodbridge office. Both gave the Trust every opportunity to run stories and articles in the only major local daily in Suffolk. Indeed John would often ring me and ask me if I would like him to hear what I was saying today about the county's big issues. He was so good at prompting me to get into a story. It soon became obvious that this publicity would be very productive in attracting new members to our organisation.

We had regular meetings trying to plan stories, and when desperate we thought up something to put in the public domain. On one occasion when particularly struggling for ideas we were sitting around the picnic table in the garden at the then HQ. An earwig ran across the table and somebody enquired as to how many species of earwigs existed in Suffolk. Ears pricked up and a call was made to the Suffolk Biological Records Centre at the Ipswich Museum. There were apparently three species in Suffolk of which two species were common but the third had not been recorded in recent years.

We sat down and constructed a press release which was headed: "Where is the missing earwig?" The outcome was extraordinary. Not only was the earwig discovered to still be alive and well in Suffolk, but the story was picked up well outside the county. It ran on BBC TV's John Craven's *Newsround* and amazingly I did pieces for Radio Japan and a radio station in Toronto, Canada. This illustrated the power of the press and how it could be used to assist in our work.

I still believe that an organisation's profile is so important. We forget that not everybody is a joiner, but by having a good profile people know what the organisation stands for and what it is doing. The following is a good example of how that might work. It was an article in the *East Anglian Daily Times* that led to the Trust being left the lovely Grove Farm, which is such an asset in demonstrating how profitable farming and wildlife can exist together. The owners' solicitor saw an article on SWT work and called me, asking if we might be prepared to accept the farm as a legacy once the owner was no longer with us. They had tried to get the National Trust to take it but they considered the property too small. It was the newspaper article that led the solicitor to call.

This also emphasises the importance of legacies to charities. There are lots of grants available but you still have to find matched funding. Grants are usually aligned with projects and so you can end up with an organisation that I could best compare with a polo mint. Lots of activity around the edges but nothing at the heart of the charity. Legacy income is generally unspecific and is able to be used to fund the core activity and to build up a substantial cash reserve. This means that if a parcel of threatened land needs to be purchased you can do so and replenish the coffers later. There are good recent examples of how the Suffolk Wildlife Trust has done just that.

I had also dabbled a bit in local radio. Before joining the Trust I had done a couple of things about birds in the county on the commercial station Radio Orwell. Later I would do a number of news pieces on this station. Eventually, though, the BBC arrived in town to be part of the regional network of stations all around the UK. The boss of the new BBC Radio Suffolk was Ivan Howlett, a 'Suffolk Boy', who was returning to his home area to get the whole project moving. Somehow Ivan found me and my involvement with the BBC began. I remember doing a piece on the work of SWT on the inaugural programme and was followed into the studio by the media's self-appointed moral judge Mary Whitehouse. I do not think I left her anything to complain about.

This relationship with the BBC grew and grew. I soon found myself doing regular weekly slots on Suffolk wildlife and also a number of recorded nature walks with Chris Opperman which went out on Saturday mornings. There were also some special programmes as well. I well remember

The author broadcasting with Chris Opperman of BBC Radio Suffolk

one which highlighted the importance of our estuaries and the hordes of birds present there in winter. I persuaded Bill Oddie to spend a day with me and Chris Opperman out on the River Alde, where we reported on wildlife during each hour of the tide cycle. We would report in live, and in between in the studio various users of the waterway contributed their thoughts as well.

It was soon after that the Ivan Howlett asked me to Chair the BBC Radio Suffolk Advisory Council, which I did for a number of years and which also saw me more involved with the BBC at regional level. Our relationship with BBC and Anglia TV had also grown and our work regularly featured on items in the evening news programmes. By now many of the SWT staff were extremely professional in using the media and our profile grew and grew.

During this time Ivan Howlett came up with a great idea of re-establishing a programme on national radio along the lines of *Nature Parliament*. This was a programme from my youth where a panel answered listener's questions on wildlife. The outcome of this brainwave was *Home Planet,* presented by Richard Daniel and produced by Nick Patrick and later Toby Murcott, which dealt with a much broader number of environmental questions and on which I was proud to be a panel member. The show ran on BBC Radio 4 for 12 years before being sadly scrapped in 2011.

During those heady years I had got to know many of the well-known people who promoted birds and other wildlife in the media. Quite early on I had the pleasure of meeting Sir David Attenborough. He was conducting a lecture tour throughout the UK in aid of the British Wildlife Appeal. During his visit to Ipswich we shared an hour or two in Bradfield Woods. We met again on several occasions during my nature conservation career and I always found him a most agreeable and informative companion. I did have to confess to him, though, that I had to watch his programmes several times to appreciate the full content. His soporific voice often made me fall asleep during watching.

Professor David Bellamy was a great friend of The Wildlife Trusts and a wonderful motivator as well. I often

The author with David Bellamy in the early days of working for Suffolk Wildlife Trust

met David and he was particularly supportive with the restoration project at Redgrave and Lopham Fen where he had carried out botanical studies for his PhD. I had known Bill Oddie since those early bird races and nobody was more supportive than Bill during my Wildlife Trust life. He would readily come and open events, new nature reserves and so on to ensure we got lots of publicity, but more than that he is a true friend and we have spent many happy hours watching birds at home and abroad.

I first met Chris Packham in a ditch at Santon Downham. At the time it was the last-known place in the UK to have a breeding pair of Red-backed Shrikes. I was checking up on the site when I discovered this young, leather-clad, peroxide punk. The suspicious side of me deduced that he must be up to no good so I quizzed him hard about why he was there, completely ignoring his binoculars. He explained that being a Hampshire lad he was passionate about Red-backed Shrikes and had volunteered to Ron Hoblyn at the Forestry Commission to spend some time watching over these rare birds. There started another friendship. A year or two later my kids pointed out this whacky guy on *The Really Wild Show* on TV and there was Chris again. He too has been a great support over the years, helping to draw attention to projects that I have been involved with.

There have been others too. Nick Baker has always obliged when asked to help out and has remained a staunch supporter of Wildlife Watch, the junior branch of The Wildlife Trusts. Much more recently The Urban Birder David Lindo and *The One Show*'s bubbling Mike Dilger have also become good friends.

Others I did not really know well also came to my aid when asked. Sir Richard Branson came to Foxburrow Farm to launch a project; Michael Palin rose to the occasion in a memorable way when he opened the new SWT headquarters at Brooke House, Ashbocking; Paul Heiney, who lived locally, also got involved; and Percy Edwards, that mimic of birds and grandfather clocks, came to our aid on a couple of occasions. All their efforts were much appreciated as they helped a great deal to raise the profile and give credibility to what we were trying to do.

The author with Michael Palin at the opening of the SWT headquarters at Ashbocking

It was in 1990, after the Berlin Wall was fractured and regimes changed, that I ventured to eastern Poland and met up for the first time with my now great friend Marek Borkowski. Marek was already well known in the UK for his work, in particular for protecting the lekking sites of Great Snipe in his home country. Marek also showed me one of his essential management tools – his herd of Tarpan or Konik horses. The Tarpan was the temperate European wild horse, but the species had become extinct in the wild. Careful breeding from domestic stock showing characteristics of the wild animal has produced the Konik. It is a useful animal for conservation management purposes as it grazes and browses

Konik horses grazing a Suffolk fen – ideal for marshland management

emerging vegetation and maintains wetland meadows and fens in a favourable condition. Being a very hardy animal it generally requires minimum veterinary attention.

As soon as the Redgrave and Lopham Fen Project was complete I arranged with Marek to obtain a stallion and four pregnant mares, and these were the first Koniks to arrive in the UK to graze our wetlands. Chris Packham led the first animal from the horse box to the reserve. Quite a few horsey people objected to their arrival, claiming that British breeds would do the same job. I was not convinced and it was very helpful to have the support of the Duke of Edinburgh, who paid a private visit to the site and then came and opened the new visitor centre which was paid for with Heritage Lottery Funds. The day before the opening I was sitting enjoying

The author with Prince Philip and Marek Borkowski at Redgrave and Lopham Fen

a cup of coffee as a Greenish Warbler sang above my head. How fitting that a breeding bird of the Biebrza Marshes in Poland had paid a visit to our reserve, where Konik horses from the same place were grazing peacefully.

Soon the RSPB and others were realising the value of Koniks and now they can be seen grazing on many British wetland nature reserves.

It was around this time that a challenging situation presented itself. While I was out of the country a member of the SWT Senior Team approached a Trustee under false pretences and demanded that I be removed as Director. He alleged that he represented the staff. On my return a hurriedly arranged Executive Meeting was put together and I offered my resignation if I was deemed to be a problem.

Apparently all but one of the Senior Team felt I was moving the Trust in the wrong direction. I later discovered that these people had been planning this action for up to a year.

The people at the meeting gave me their full support and conducted a survey of other staff and key members to find that this view was only shared by the five senior staff. The personnel involved all left the SWT's employment within six months. Julian Roughton, the then Conservation Officer, and whose loyalty to me was obvious from the start, assisted with support of the Trustees in rebuilding the Senior Team very quickly and the Trust has gone from strength to strength. Since 1999 Julian has been its Director.

This was a daunting experience and flagged up one of the problems with people working in nature conservation. Most then had never worked in a 'business situation' and in my case felt that final decisions should be taken by staff on a sort of consensus basis, rather than by Trustees and the Director. I always felt I had listened to arguments by staff, but at the end of the day it had to be my call.

What was impressive throughout this trauma was the enormous support of the Council and Executive and the loyalty of the rest of the staff. Every Chairman I worked with was absolutely first class, but I must pay particular tribute to Hugh Philbrick. Hugh served with me for six years, and through some of the more challenging times. He never took his eye off the ball and stood firmly behind me and all the staff. He and I were from such different backgrounds yet we seemed to not only have a great working relationship but also became good friends. My only regret is that I was on the other side of the world in Australia when he died and I could not be at his funeral.

Trustees were really supportive and some have left me with wonderful stories. I recall the ageing Edgar Milne-Redhead being sound asleep in a Council Meeting. The Chairman wickedly asked him to comment on the matter being discussed. Edgar awoke immediately and said "I agree with the last chap." William Jacob, a good friend of Hugh Philbrick and ex-Fleet Air Arm Officer, stunned an Executive Committee Meeting. A member of staff had tabled a paper asking for a discussion on whether to introduce stress management sessions for staff. William opened the debate with a long tirade on being shot down in Korea, being captured, escaping and then going back for another go at the enemy. He suggested this had been a perfect solution to stress. The Chairman promptly moved on the next item on the agenda and the matter was never tabled again.

Things quickly moved on and we were soon involved in many exciting projects. Thanks to the generosity of owners Robin and Tim Miller we had purchased Foxburrow Farm at Melton where, amongst other things, we had set up an educational team to receive as many school children as possible. This meant involving the kids in games which explained our relationship with the natural world. Again it was a fairly new thing for a Wildlife Trust but I had long been persuaded that educating as many people as possible was much more effective than buying more and more nature reserves. We had by now also built the visitor centre at Carlton Marshes and were encouraging similar activity in the Lowestoft area.

Foxburrow Farm also became the headquarters for the trust's 'flying' flock of sheep. Suffolk has very few livestock nowadays and animals were needed particularly to graze heathland. With money received from winning the UK Ford Conservation Award the Trust purchased a flock of Beulah Ewes with a couple of Leicester and a Suffolk ram. As well as meeting a management need, the sheep proved popular with the public and an annual lambing day soon became a regular event. The public was asked to sponsor and then name their ewe and some hilarious names came forward. I particularly remember 'Ba-ba Jacket' and 'Bababababarbara Ann'.

Later we added more sheep in the form of the tougher Hebridean breed. This was made possible by somebody calling at the office and offering a ram and some ewes in exchange for a Life Membership of the Trust.

Another ground-breaking project was the two midweek teams running from Lowestoft and Ipswich. These, complete with their own minibuses and supervisors, picked up people who were unemployed, retired, or otherwise available to work during the daytime, and took them to do vital management work on wildlife sites in Suffolk.

I pause here to record two sad losses in my life. First my dear mother passed away at the age of 78 after a series of health problems. Mother had never really understood what I did for a living since joining the SWT. She did realise that it made me very happy and she loved seeing me occasionally on the regional TV news. I do not think that she paid much attention to what I was saying, but she would point out if my hair was too long or I was not wearing a tie. I know she was proud of me even if she did once suggest that maybe I should consider getting a proper job. It was the end of an era.

The other great sadness was that my great friend Brian Brown was diagnosed with bone cancer in 1999. Brian was a very big man in many ways and it was a devastating experience to see him deteriorate so fast. In the last conversation I had with Brian he had two regrets – one that he had not travelled enough in search of birds and secondly that he was going to miss the Millennium. Meeting Brian and his wife Christine was one of the most influential moments of my life. I was delighted, while twitching a Hume's Warbler in Lowestoft recently, to meet up with Brian's son, Tim Brown. Brian would be so chuffed that he is carrying on the birding tradition. There are many stories I could tell about Brian, but the one that stands out is what happened after we had seen our first White-tailed Eagle at Sizewell in Suffolk. Brian did not have an exceptional education but he could best be described as a self-taught intellectual who appreciated opera and classical music. He looked down his nose at me playing anything lighter. Anyway, he called me after I got home and said "have you ticked it yet?" I assumed he meant had I put the bird on my life list. "No" I replied. "Right" said Brian "I am going to put on a record of Elgar's *Pomp and Circumstance* and you must wait until it reaches a crescendo and then we must both tick it simultaneously." Well we did and Brian pointed out later that such a bird simply could not be added to a list in any other way. What a great guy – I miss him a great deal.

Birds still drove my enthusiasm but I made a point of not twitching while working and this did mean I missed a few good species in my native county. The ability to actually do more for birds made up for missing the occasional rarity. One such opportunity was the chance to acquire part of my beloved Walberswick, an area where I had learnt so much in my early days. The southern part of the massive area of reedbeds and the shore pools all the way to Dunwich were being offered for sale. It was a massive chance to bring this valuable land into conservation ownership and management.

The asking price of a million pounds was a little beyond the means of SWT in those days, so after some early sparring I persuaded the RSPB to consider a joint purchase. At the time this was a very radical suggestion. Richard

Powell, the Regional Officer of the RSPB, seemed to be in broad agreement so we pressed on together. Much of the success in achieving this aim was down to the then SWT Reserves Manager, Nick Collinson, who collated a massive application to submit to the Heritage Lottery Fund and to the Earl of Cranbrook for ensuring that we received a quick response.

Dingle Marshes is now a joint Suffolk Wildlife Trust/RSPB reserve

Obviously there were teething problems with such a new concept, and egos had to be massaged in both organisations before it began to work smoothly. Now this significant reserve is managed and owned jointly and my only regret is that Natural England, or English Nature as they were known then, did not agree to include the northern portion of Walberswick and Westleton Heath into one large National

Nature Reserve managed as one. In my opinion this is still a missed opportunity.

By now I had spent 14 years at SWT and was wondering where I went next. These thoughts were interrupted by a serious spine problem. Years of abusing my body on the sports fields of East Anglia had finally caught up with me. My sciatic nerve was trapped by a slipped disc and it took two major operations to correct the problem and get me walking properly again. Spending quite a lot of time on a motorised buggy gave me a new insight into peoples' attitudes to the 'disabled' as well.

It was at this time in my career that Beryl and I received an invitation to attend a garden party at Buckingham Palace. This was a bit of a surprise, but off we went dressed up in our Sunday best. It was a strange experience as we were whisked quickly out onto the lawns at the rear of the palace amongst the 2,000 or so other guests. We knew that we would not be meeting any of the royal family on that day so were reasonably relaxed. And we were able to observe the extraordinary behaviour of some people, using techniques which would be more at home in a rugby match, to get themselves as close to the royal party as possible so they could give themselves a chance of touching royal gloved hands.

When the royal party went into their tent for tea I was even more astonished when the same people sat in rows of seats just watching them sipping their Earl Grey and

The author and his wife, Beryl, at the Buckingham Palace garden party

nibbling their cucumber sandwiches. It reminded me of the chimpanzees' tea party at London Zoo. The highlight for me was being able walk around the lake in the gardens and look at the collection of pinioned wildfowl, which included some splendid Ruddy Shelducks. I was also impressed when I flushed a Eurasian Sparrowhawk out of a small shrubbery.

Afterwards, as we walked out of the palace gates, we were waylaid by some American girls who asked who we were. We explained that we were nobody important but had just enjoyed tea with the Queen (a slight exaggeration) and they found it hard to believe that ordinary folks could go and wander around the monarch's backyard and enjoy a cup of tea. They insisted on photographing us and explaining that such a thing could never happen in The White House.

A year after this a small brown envelope dropped through my letterbox one Saturday morning. It was from 10 Downing Street, announcing that my name had been put forward to the Queen recommending me for an OBE. The letter specifically said that I would receive the honour "should she be minded" and that would find out if this was so on 31st December 1998. This was quite a shock because I had no inkling that this was going to happen.

Well Her Majesty was "minded" and I was deluged with calls from the East Anglian media on that day. I, of course, also received a lot of letters of congratulations from across the spectrum of people I had worked with over the years. What was more interesting was the letters that I did not receive. Obviously many disapproved of the honours system or indeed of me receiving one. You know who you are!

It was a great honour for me and for my family, who had been most supportive and deserved most of the credit for the award. It was also considerable recognition of the Suffolk

The author with daughter Bronwen at the Buckingham Palace investiture

Wildlife Trust and all the staff and members who had played such a part in the organisation's growth and success.

My day at Buckingham Palace was very memorable and I was accompanied by my wife Beryl and daughter Bronwen. It was not just the excitement of meeting Her Majesty the Queen but the fact that I stood in line for over an hour next to Welsh singer Tom Jones. The conversations with Tom will always remain with me.

My next step in life also became apparent at this time, when there was a need for somebody to take up a position at the Royal Society of Wildlife Trusts heading up the Conservation Department. The previous incumbent had decided to leave very suddenly and I was contacted and asked if I would consider taking it on. Suffolk farmer John Cousins was already working in that team and he was instrumental in persuading me to take up the challenge, at first on a secondment basis in January 1999.

It was also obvious that the Suffolk Wildlife Trust was now able to move forward with someone else at the helm, and indeed it probably needed a change of style and direction.

Starting work in a central position within the Wildlife Trusts was something completely different. I have already alluded to the tensions that existed between the 47 separate charities and the centre. Legally the centre can only work in a co-ordinating role but various egos had often tried to present the centre as more than that. Any attempt to assume a leadership role was bound to encounter problems.

In the three years I worked at the centre I found my task almost impossible. When I arrived morale amongst the staff was at rock bottom. I hope I did at least manage to improve that situation. By the time I left in 2001 I think that some people were smiling again. There were many terrible problems to deal with whilst I was there. A senior Director had apparently misled everybody about the financial situation and worse had behaved most inappropriately. Needless to say he soon disappeared from the scene. This cast the organisation into complete chaos and most efforts then were concentrated on reassessing the finances and revisiting priorities. It was a very bad time and the situation was not helped by a Chief

Executive who was very able in public relations but behaved like an ostrich in respect of everything else.

I did, however, enjoy my relationship with the 47 Wildlife Trusts and was now in a position to visit many of them on their territory and take part in discussing their various plans. One which stands out as a seminal moment was when, with Nick Hammond and Brian Eversham of the Wildlife Trust for Bedfordshire, Cambridgeshire and Northamptonshire, we visited Home Fen and Woodwalton Fen. Our purpose was to discuss the feasibility of what is now known as The Great Fen Project. It has become hugely successful and has laid down markers for all of those wanting to create large and feasible areas for nature conservation.

I was also asked to visit a few Wildlife Trusts to speak at their AGMs, with the emphasis on a talk entitled 'Are our Nature Reserves Too Small?' I used this to challenge our previous thoughts on acquiring land. Using my experiences from Eastern Europe I was keen to get the Wildlife Trusts to think bigger. Many WT reserves then were mere pin-pricks on the landscape and I urged them to consider making strategic purchases to join up and link areas to create bigger tracts of habitat. This discussion was the forerunner of the Wildlife Trusts' 'Living Landscapes' project today.

Visiting other Wildlife Trusts also opened my eyes to the vast amount of very imaginable work being carried out to create an interest in wildlife. I realised that you can develop very polarised views through working in just one area of the UK. I was amazed by the project with Bangladeshi women and their allotments in Bolton, the extraordinary Bog Meadows project in Belfast, and the efforts of the London Wildlife Trust when they had little chance of ever owning significant areas of land.

It was during this time that I also paid visits to Wales, where there were many challenges to get the Wildlife Trusts there to work together and present themselves as a united group to the fairly newly devolved Welsh Assembly.

With life internally at RSWT now being impossible for me I was so glad to be offered an escape route by some of the Wildlife Trusts in Wales. As a family we had spent many memorable holidays in west Wales, so the thought of going to live there held no fears. Indeed we were excited by the idea.

In July 2001 I moved down to Wales to take on yet another challenge. During my time with the Trusts it was obvious that those in Wales were punching well below their weight. Only the West Wales Wildlife Trust was really well known, and then mainly because of its management of those wonderful islands Skomer and Skokholm. West Wales was the main reason for my involvement because I already had friends in that area and the Trust was in dire financial trouble, having been tainted by their Chief Executive and the RSWT Director already mentioned.

I was convinced to pick up my life and move to Wales

mainly thanks to the persuasive powers of Roy Jones, the then Chairman of the Glamorgan Wildlife Trust. Roy is a true Welshman and was enthusiastic that at least West Wales, Glamorgan and Gwent should merge as one Wildlife Trust. He also shared a vision that all Welsh Wildlife Trusts should merge to form one powerful body for Wales. It made sense, particularly as many of the Trusts in Wales were so small that the oft-mentioned fact that they had more sheep in their counties than people was true.

West Wales was in dire need of help as it was on the verge of bankruptcy. This was a fact accepted by the then Chairman David Gardner and trustee and friend Jack Donovan. Sadly this was not recognised by many of the members, and worst of all by some stubborn Trustees. Doing nothing was not an option.

At that time Glamorgan was run in a very old-fashioned way which was very similar to many of the Trusts during my early days. Management was carried out by a loose group of trustees who did not necessarily have any management experience. A merger was right for those two Trusts at least.

This was not the case for Gwent. They had just appointed an enthusiastic young Director in Julian Branscomb and felt they needed to bed down the organisation using their existing resources before thinking about a merger. In my opinion that was a sensible decision and frankly I could not have coped initially with their involvement.

The next year or so was very difficult. Some staff
members, particularly those having received little direct
management, were very demotivated and sadly some had to
leave. Significant debts had to be addressed just to keep the
new body alive. Some large projects, like the restoration at
Skomer, were reactivated and the Trust moved on under its
new name The Wildlife Trust for South and West Wales.

I received a great deal of support from many people across
Wales and we managed to stave off going under and kept

Red-billed Choughs are characteristic birds of the Pembrokeshire islands

our heads above water. The Countryside Council for Wales,
led by CEO Roger Thomas, was particularly supportive in

making sure that the Trust had enough funds to keep moving on. The sad passing of the iconic Ronald Lockley provided a legacy which also helped a great deal.

Frankly the job had become very stressful and a small minority of prominent members were making my job very difficult. One senior member of the Trust turned out to be a disaster and the finances were not significantly improving. My efforts to get all the Welsh Trusts to form a single national Trust were getting nowhere. The staff seemed to like the idea but trustees were at best cautious, with many being totally against it. I felt for the first time in my nature conservation career that I had failed. My health was definitely being affected so I decided to call it a day.

I had always made it clear that I would only work for three years and try to achieve the merger. I knew that I would upset too many people by staying longer. So in 2004 I stood down and handed over to Dr Madeleine Havard, who had worked with me for most of my time in Wales.

Today the excellent Sarah Kessell, who I had enticed to Wales as Conservation Officer, is the Chief Executive. Although finances remain tight the Trust is still in existence and has achieved great things. Madeleine and Sarah managed the purchase of Skokholm when it eventually came onto the market (it had previously been leased) and Sarah more recently has purchased the lighthouse and land on Skokholm from Trinity House. A parallel achievement had been to encourage an army of volunteers to get involved in the restoration of the buildings on the island and hopefully restart what was Britain's first-ever Bird Observatory.

At a time when I was totally immersed in my wonderful job a near tragedy occurred and I was brought back down to earth with a big bang. I had been in Great Yarmouth on a Friday night talking to the local RSPB group, and had spent the Saturday birding with locals on the Norfolk coast before returning home to Boxted that evening. As I drove up to the house there were no lights on and the place looked unlived in. It was now beginning to snow and the house was cold. My wife Beryl had been slightly unwell earlier in the week and her doctor had diagnosed bronchitis.

I immediately went upstairs to find my wife very ill. She had apparently been like this for 24 hours and could now only crawl to the bathroom. I immediately called the doctor who still insisted that she only had bronchitis and did not sound as if she was coming to our aid as the weather was so bad. I was very concerned but within half an hour the doorbell rang. There was a young man with a bag who introduced himself as Dr David Milne. He went immediately to my wife, took a blood sample, disappeared and returned quickly afterwards urging me to prepare for my wife to be taken to hospital.

By now the weather was atrocious with deep snow and

more coming. The doctor had summoned an army unit with some sort of vehicle which whisked my wife off to Colchester Hospital. I was left alone worrying like mad. Later that evening I learnt that Beryl had suffered a complete kidney failure and was being rushed to the Royal London Hospital. I was distraught and so concerned that I found myself telephoning friends at 2 o'clock in the morning. The next day good friend Melvyn Eke came with a Land Rover and took me to the Royal London Hospital. Beryl was now in good hands and a kind and sympathetic consultant spent two hours explaining what was happening. His news was not good. Beryl's kidney failure was almost 100 per cent and she required dialysis every day. Even if she improved a lot she might need this for the rest of her life. There were no dialysis facilities except in London in those days so he said that I would have to consider giving up my job, selling my house and finding cheaper accommodation so I could buy a dialysis machine and spend my time caring for Beryl. This was shattering news.

I had good birding friend, Edward Keeble, living in Greenwich, which is not far from the hospital, and he and his wonderful wife Camilla insisted I could stay with them during the week so that I could visit Beryl daily. This I did for nearly three months and it was towards the end of this period that the consultant called me into his office again. He explained that Beryl was responding so well to treatment that he now thought she might eventually be able to manage without daily dialysis. In fact he said she was so fit and determined that she might not need dialysis at all.

Well the rest is now history. Beryl made an amazing recovery and within a year returned to leading a pretty normal life. So much so that both our attitudes to life changed quite a bit. We realized that nothing was more important than life itself and began to think more about how to live. This meant an element of throwing caution to the wind and starting to travel and see more of our amazing world. Our gratitude to David Milne and the staff at the Royal London Hospital will never be forgotten.

It was during my career with the Wildlife Trusts that the British Birdwatching Fair was born. Now known to most simply as 'Birdfair', it was the brainchild of Tim Appleton, the Manager of Rutland Water Nature Reserve (which is run by the Leicestershire and Rutland Wildlife Trust) and Martin Davies of the RSPB. The site is owned by Anglian Water and it too has played its part in making this event so successful. I did not attend the first Birdfair as I could not see how the idea would catch on. Now, with the event's 25th anniversary taking place in 2013, Birdfair is enormous and reaches out in a completely global way.

It is hard to know where to start in appreciation of this major annual event. I have attended all the Birdfairs except for that first one and I have been delighted to be allowed to take part and assist in its growth in a small way. I got formally involved in the early days by taking over the organisation of the Big County Bird Race, which took place each spring and raised a substantial contribution to the year's total. The Bird Race lasted quite a few years but eventually faded away as people saw better and greener ways to use their energies.

By now, though, I was completely hooked and one of my first contributions was to get the RSWT to appear at the

The Wildlife Trusts campaigning for marine conservation issues at The British Birdwatching Fair at Rutland Water

Birdfair on behalf of all the Wildlife Trusts. In the early days it was difficult to motivate HQ staff, but I was supported by many people from East Anglian Trusts and to this day RSWT maintains a significant presence at the event. This was important to me, especially since a Wildlife Trust is one of the joint organisers and the event takes place on one of the Trust's reserves.

The event grew and grew and I found myself agreeing to do all sorts of things, from 20-minute talks on various subjects to full-blown entertainment events on the main stage. This meant working with a plethora of people like Bill Oddie, Chris Packham, Mike Dilger, Nick Baker, Stephen Moss and many other well-known birders. These events are very much part of the scene at Birdfair and this includes the 'Bird Brain of Britain' competition which I eventually managed to win in 2000.

I have found myself doing all sorts of other enjoyable things too, including refereeing the seven-a-side football tournament which was a feature of the fair for many years. Nowadays I think all the players have got too old, and the referees too, so this competition has ceased. However, it does show that the event is constantly evolving and could easily now be described as the International Birdfair. From memory exhibitors now come from the USA, Argentina, Ecuador, Peru, Colombia, Costa Rica, Trinidad and Tobago, Panama, Finland, The Netherlands, France, Estonia, Spain, Greece,

Bird Brain of Britain 2000 – Champion at last

Poland, Bulgaria, Malta, South Africa, Uganda, Gambia, Kazakhstan, Israel, India, Sri Lanka, Malaysia, Taiwan, Australia and New Zealand.

It is no surprise that some of the inspiration to get me travelling in search of birds has come from Birdfair. For example, my first trip to India was organised by Leio and Jennifer De Souza of Indian Nature Tours, and my visit to Brazil by Xavier Muñoz-Contreras of Neblina Forest Tours. All of whom I met at Birdfair.

In addition, over the years I have regularly met up with old friends and made lots of new ones too. It is a tremendous social event and an opportunity to learn so much as well. A chance to try out new optics and glance at and purchase the latest books and gismos. Most of all, it is an opportunity to have a great time and also to raise big and meaningful sums of money for conservation projects all over the world. Tim and Martin deserve enormous praise for having thought this gem up, but more importantly keeping it going and keeping it growing for a quarter of a century.

6.

Travelling for Birds

Working for the Wildlife Trusts also produced some opportunities to travel. The Norfolk and Suffolk Wildlife Trusts decided to set up a holiday company to offer wildlife trips to our members. These were mostly to destinations in Europe, and profits would go to the 10 per cent requirement to unlock Landfill Tax funds for conservation work. The highly industrious Anne Cryer organised these events and I was able to lead trips to Crete, Cyprus, Spain, Morocco, Gambia, Costa Rica and North America. I had already led trips to Holland, Poland and North America with the Field Studies Council.

Leading wildlife holidays was a completely new

experience and not without difficulties. People go on such holidays for a complex number of reasons. Some are unashamed twitchers, even if it is only for two weeks a year. As soon as you show them one species they want to press on with the next almost immediately. Their list seems to be the thing they most want to take home. Single men and woman seem to be looking for company, which is reasonable enough, but one lady several years my senior did shake me by suggesting that I might like to move in with her. She was deeply upset when I explained that I was married. She could not believe that a married man would be allowed to run around the world taking people birdwatching.

I enjoyed, and still do enjoy, showing people wildlife and sharing in the experience, but what I did find hard was being everything to everyone. I did get asked some extraordinary questions. One lady called me just before a North American trip to enquire as to how much underwear she should pack. I was rendered speechless. Many who have travelled with me know that my favourite gripe is postcards. Imagine you are in the deserts of eastern Jordan when somebody asks you "where can we buy postcards." Do they think you just flag down a passing Bedouin? True, such things can be bought at places like Petra, but then where can you get the relevant stamp and where do you post it?

It seems amazing to me that people will spend a small fortune on going to some exotic parts of the world to see wildlife and the one thing that worries them for the two weeks is sending someone a postcard. I was leading a trip to the Pyrénées with Norfolk wildlife photographer Roger Tidman. A particular client was going on and on about posting his cards. This went on for a couple of days and we never really saw any postboxes. Finally one afternoon Roger suddenly stopped the minibus and grabbed the cards. He walked across a village street and popped them through a letterbox in a large door beside a church. The client was delighted that his cards were at last off his hands. Later I asked Roger if he thought that the door belonged to a post office. He declared he had no idea but that he could not stand the complaining any more.

The extraordinary outcome of this story is that I saw the client concerned a year later and asked him if his friends received their postcards okay. "Oh yes," he said, "they were all very pleased". I have this vision of some poor Spaniard finding the cards on his doormat and diligently taking them to the nearest postbox.

Most of my early trips abroad were to The Netherlands. Being so close geographically, it was easy to get ferries from Felixstowe or Harwich and just go for a long weekend. Our early efforts were all courtesy of the kindness of Dutch birding friends that I had met during the old bird race days. Gerald Oreel kindly tolerated four or five of us sleeping all over his Amsterdam flat. We would then join up with others, especially the late Jowi de Roever, and just go birding. We mostly visited in winter when we could enjoy the hordes of wildfowl present there. We could also be sure of finding Black Woodpecker, Crested Lark, Short-toed Treecreeper and Crested Tit – all species that we were not likely to see in Suffolk.

This was also the time when Great White Egrets were beginning to nest on the polders, so we could add that species to our list as well. These were wonderful times even though driving in The Netherlands was sometimes a bit terrifying for poor old John Grant. Later my son Jeremy went to work for Shell and lived in Groningen for four years so my visits increased. It was also at this time that I started running birding weekends to The Netherlands. I always did this with birding pal Dougal Urqhart. We always stayed at a hotel in Harderwijk which was owned by our great friends Adriaan and Aileen Schouten. This was a great place to stay and was within easy reach of all the best birding spots, with many interesting species to be found in the woods surrounding the hotel. I continued to use this place for many other visits, including a Wildlife Trusts Directors' Conference. Sadly, just as Adriaan retired a year or two ago he was diagnosed with cancer and tragically died. We are still touch with Aileen and their daughter Gwendoline.

It was during all this activity that I visited one particular site many times. I was hooked on Oostvaardersplassen on the

The massive Oostvaardersplassen wetland reserve in The Netherlands

polder of South Flevoland, just to the south of the town of Lelystad. Here was a project of modern habitat creation that inspired me then and has continued to excite me ever since. The Netherlands, of course, is one of the few countries that has increased its land area in recent times. When reclaiming the land in the Zuider Zee and creating the polders, scattering phragmites seeds was part of the plan. This is how Oostvaardersplassen came to be.

As the polder was being developed, the 6,000-hectare site was set aside as an industrial area but it quickly grew up to be a pristine reedbed. Because of this it became a fantastic area for wildlife, and especially for birds. It was also a significant green lung between the new towns of Lelystad and Almere.

The outcome was that before any development could take place the people of these towns demanded that it be kept as a nature reserve. The Dutch Government agreed and the State Forestry Department, Staatsbosbeheer, was given the task of creating and managing what we have today.

Frans Vera is the architect of this great place and I have been lucky to meet him, and also to be encouraged by others like Vincent Wigbels and Hans Kampf. This huge area of wetland and grassland is now like a European Serengeti. In the early days thousands of moulting Greylag Geese from further north descended on the site and began to graze the grass and the rhizomes of the reeds. Their presence created a different mosaic of wetland habitats and encouraged a more diverse array of species. This led to large herbivores being introduced in the form of Heck cattle (a non-domestic form bred in Leipzig Zoo to represent the aurochs), Konik horses and Red Deer. These now number about 3,000 in total and live as wild animals with as little intervention as possible. The large mammals are natural managers and have, together with the geese, created a stunning landscape and mosaic of habitats.

Oostvaardersplassen's avifauna is remarkable. In winter there are thousands of geese, including Greylag, White-fronted, Bean and Barnacle. Huge numbers of ducks and waders also congregate here. The star duck at this time is the Smew. Hundreds spend the winter, and if they are not on the

Greylag Geese colonised Oostvaardersplassen both to carry out moult and to nest, and their grazing created a mosaic of wetland habitats

reserve then they will certainly be around Lelystad Harbour and on the Markermeer. Raptors are very numerous with Rough-legged Buzzard, Hen Harrier and Northern Goshawk all common at this season. Even more exciting has been the regular occurrence of White-tailed Eagle, a pair of which has now begun to nest annually on the reserve. Rare raptors include occasional Great Spotted Eagles and once even a Black Vulture.

During the summer this vast wetland is full of nesting birds, including hundreds of pairs of Savi's Warblers, Marsh Warblers and White-spotted Bluethroats. Eurasian and Little Bitterns, Purple Herons, Great White Egrets and Eurasian Spoonbills also breed in this vast area, while other reedbed species include Bearded and Penduline Tits. The number of Marsh Harriers nesting here is huge and a few Montagu's Harriers occur in agricultural fields on them margins of the reserve. Many migrants and vagrants also occur.

What is so inspirational is the reserve's sheer size. There are plans to link it up with other reserves nearby and create an area of 15,000 hectares totally devoted to nature conservation. The plans then include linking this up to the Veluwe on the mainland and then to other areas as far as the German border. The Dutch Government is actively planning that Lynx and Wolf should be enticed back to their country

The Dutch Government is encouraging large mammals like the Wolf to return to the country through creating corridors of suitable habitat

by entering through these corridors.

Now if a country which is so small and which has a population of 17 million people can do this, then why on earth cannot we in the UK replicate such plans? I will tell you why. Not only would any UK Government not have the guts to do such a thing, much worse still I believe that a great number of purist conservationists would decry such a move. I have taken hundreds of people to see this reserve and most are very impressed. I believe that we have to start emulating this effort. Maybe we should stop thinking about the past and start creating sites with a 21st century fauna and flora. I am a strong advocate for this in the UK and I know that Bert Axell would have been too.

Travelling abroad also gave me more opportunities to fight for birds. Bill Oddie and I had led a couple of birdwatching tours out to Cyprus and we had become pretty familiar with the Greek part of the island. We had enjoyed some modest success with birds and on one occasion had found the first Eastern Mourning Wheatear for the island. A more unpleasant side of this Mediterranean paradise is the widespread killing of migrant birds. It took place on a large scale, with apparently every red-blooded male dressing like Rambo just to go out and slaughter birds such as Blackcaps to eat for supper. Some of it is even worse than that.

I have seen murderous gunners with automatic shotguns shooting down flocks of European Bee-eaters, and on one occasion a guy shooting swifts. I must concede that the latter must have been one hell of a shot. In those days BirdLife International was ineffective in Cyprus and the RSPB had no resources or policy to intervene. Bill and I were approached on one of our trips by Friends of the Earth Cyprus. Its members were local people who were horrified at the killing, and in particular at the shooting of birds in spring. What made them so angry was that the practice had been made illegal by a left-wing President, but when he lost the job the new incumbent, a right-winger who was supported by hunters, had immediately restored spring shooting to the statute book. We were asked to help.

They wanted us to stir up things in the UK and put together a petition of signatures from people who opposed the killing. They also wanted us to persuade holiday companies to threaten to boycott the island. Finally they asked us to contact the Ministry of Defence to protest at birds being killed in the Sovereign Base Area, which is legally British territory.

We got together a petition of thousands of signatures and presented it to the Cypriot Government. We also went to see an Army Officer who was purportedly in charge of the Sovereign Bases in Cyprus. He was worse than useless. All he wanted was for us to join him drinking sherry at 10.30 in the morning and for Bill to agree to be photographed for some magazine. His excuse for doing nothing about the killing was that the locals might cut off their water and electricity.

It was so frustrating. I wrote to John Gummer, now Lord Deben, and, knowing that Cyprus was applying for entry to the European Union, thought that there might be something he could do in that regard. For a long time I was disappointed not to get a reply. Then one evening I arrived home to find we had an invitation to dinner at the Gummers. There were a number of people present, and as we went in to dinner John Gummer pointed out that I would be sitting next to the Greek European Minister for the Environment. He had given him my letter and his wife agreed with me. I suggest you talk to him over dinner was the advice.

It is amazing, is it not? After that meeting we soon heard that spring shooting had been banned again on Cyprus. Apparently the Greek Minister was related to the President of Cyprus and, guessing, I reckon he pointed out to him that continuing the shooting might affect the country's chances of entry into the European Union.

Our new pals in Friends of the Earth Cyprus were happy at the time but I have no idea what is happening there today. I do know that there is still a serious trapping and liming problem in parts of the Mediterranean and that BirdLife International and the RSPB are now on the case. This deplorable activity also still takes place in the Sovereign Base Area with the apparent blessing of the UK Government, even though it is illegal under European Law.

I should add that I exchanged letters with and then met Labour minister Peter Hain regarding using the entry of Malta into Europe as a great opportunity to stop people on this island from carrying out their illegal slaughter of migrant birds and, perhaps worse, their criminal attacks on people trying to stop them. We will wait until they are in and then we will be able to stop it was the response. Once again nothing has happened. Malta is in the European Union, everything happening regarding hunting and trapping is is illegal but little is done.

Also at this time The Wildlife Trusts was a member of Eurosite, an organisation set up to exchange management techniques and such among NGOs and government agencies throughout the European Union. The Suffolk Wildlife Trust obtained a contract to train staff from emerging NGOs from Eastern European countries after the collapse of communism and the fall of the Berlin Wall. I therefore spent time in Hungary, Poland and Slovakia running events more to help with establishing the bodies as NGOs rather than dealing with the science of nature conservation, at which the staff in these places were already adept. To assist, a number of staff from these new organisations came over to Suffolk to work with SWT staff and pick up ideas which they could take back home and apply. It was quite normal for our house to have guests from Eastern Europe in those days and we fondly remember the girls from Slovakia who we christened the Spice Girls.

This involvement was inspirational to me, not least having the opportunity to see at first hand large tracts of land which were already holding considerably more biodiversity than most of Western Europe. Of course I made time to see birds as well. I was thrilled to visit the Biebrza Marshes and Białowieża Forest in eastern Poland. These pristine habitats made me realise what a lot we have lost in the UK, but at the same time I could see how much could be restored. The marshes, with their huge numbers of breeding wildfowl, waders, raptors and other species, were so impressive but already this area was threatened not so much by development but by neglect. The forests were liable to suffer the same fate. These habitats are still impressive and I and my pal

Bill Oddie and Marek Borkowski during filming in the Biebrza Marhes, Poland

Marek Borkowski were privileged to be part of the team that produced a film of the area with Bill Oddie, which was screened as part of the *Birding with Bill Oddie* series.

At this time much of Eastern Europe was new to British naturalists and was beginning to open up. For the first time we could see that all the social flaws of the Communist system had probably accidentally been pretty good for wildlife. I was also able to enjoy birding in Hungary with it fabulous lakes, forests and the great area of the Hortobágy. Here extensive wetlands come face to face with herb-rich grassland, and is one of the few places where Great Bustards still breed.

Having first visited Poland in 1990, the next year I arranged to lead a group on a visit there. The party included a few Suffolk farmers, who were all interested in wildlife and were already farming their land with wildlife in mind. They wanted to come to Poland not only to look at birds and other wildlife, but also to see how the countryside was being farmed. Poland still had the small co-operative farms of the communist era and heavy horses were still more commonly used than tractors at that time.

It was an interesting exercise and showed how detached a lot of UK farmers had become from certain stages of the food production process. A good example of this was my good friend David Barker. At that time David was a big pig producer. He reared young animals and when they were old enough they were collected by lorry and taken to an abattoir.

His involvement was just rearing the animals, saying goodbye and starting again. We were watching dancing Common Cranes in Poland when he and his wife Claire decided to enter a farmyard and have a look around. He appeared a while later clutching Claire's arm and looking very much the worse for wear. Further investigation revealed that as they entered the yard a women had dragged a pig out of a building and promptly slit its throat. This was too much for David and he admitted that he had become detached from reality with his own animals. David did later produce the most humorous line of the trip when asked what was the best bird he had seen. Without hesitation he declared that it had to be "Three-legged Woodpecker".

Another person on that trip was Major Bill Payn, who had been one of the great collectors of specimens for museums, often working alongside the notorious Colonel Richard Meinertzhagen. Right up until his death Bill maintained that not collecting a vagrant was a great waste. I often envisaged him crawling through the legs of a horde of twitchers and taking out a rare waif with his dust shot. On this occasion I was showing everyone a White-backed Woodpecker and at one point I turned to Bill and said "You must have seen this species before?" Bill's reply made any further discussion unnecessary. "Seen it dear boy? I have collected it." Bill never killed anything, but he merely collected it or obtained it.

It would be good to see these places again over a decade later. How have these habitats stood up to the new regimes? Have western agricultural methods taken these places in the same direction as the UK? I do know that UK farmers were getting very interested in acquiring land for farming in Eastern Europe. Their presence may have sounded the end for much of what I saw in those early days.

The spectacular Wadi Rum in Jordan

On another occasion the Trust received a visit from staff from the Royal Society for the Conservation of Nature in Jordan. This included the Chief Executive Khalid Irani. They came to look at the varied work of the Trust with a view to increasing their activity beyond habitat management. The outcome was that Khalid invited Beryl and I to visit Jordan the following year. The RSCN was set up after the expedition led by Guy Mountfort in the 1960s which featured in the book *Portrait of a Desert*. King Hussein urged the setting up of the NGO to look after the large areas of his country he had assigned as Nature Reserves.

That first visit was extraordinary, and apart from seeing much of the wildlife of Jordan it also included visits to the Roman city of Jerash, the much reduced oasis at Azraq, the magic city of Petra and the impressive landscape of Wadi Rum. Needless to say I became hooked on this amazing country and led two further birdwatching trips there. One of these included the young Stephen Moss as my co-leader. We enjoyed the first part taking in the Roman city of Jerash and then moving out east to Azraq. We saw our first Moustached Warblers together and Stephen found me my first White-throated Robin. Then tragedy struck and a messenger brought us the news that Stephen's mother had died. The RSCN was marvellous and arranged to get Stephen back to Amman and on a flight back to London. It was a dreadful moment and we were thinking of the poor chap as we continued the tour on down via Dana, Petra and Wadi Rum to Aqaba. We then had to move up Wadi Arava alongside the Dead Sea and back to Amman. That incident cemented a friendship with Stephen which has continued right up until today.

In addition I went to Jordan with David Hosking so that

The world-famous buildings of the Monastery at Petra, Jordan

we could retrace the journey of Guy Mountfort's expedition, where David's father Eric Hosking was the photographer. We were accompanied by my cousin Robin Matthews, an architect who had a great desire to see Petra. This involved following their exact journey, photographing the same things and seeing what had changed. Just getting to Amman was amazingly quicker. We flew direct from London, but in the earlier years the process took much longer. Mountfort and company had to fly via Amsterdam and Athens. Also, in their day the roads were only tracks and the going was very slow. We had the advantage of travelling on tarmac roads most of the time.

It was a great experience and much had changed. Comparing the views there were many more trees than previously. These were mostly eucalyptus and conifer plantations. The biggest shock came when comparing photos from Azraq in the eastern desert. First of all the oasis has almost gone and only one or two small pools remained, although there was a major project under way which would see bigger areas created. When checking the photographs of Azraq castle, once the retreat of Lawrence of Arabia himself, we noticed that quite a lot of walls and bricks were missing. No doubt these were now incorporated into local houses.

The Rift Valley and places like Dana, Petra and Wadi Rum were not changed too much, but at the last site the lone castle on the valley floor is now surrounded by many more buildings. These were apparently built to house groups of Bedouins. The outcome is that the tribesmen and their families still live in their wonderful tents and their goats and other livestock are housed in the buildings. It was a stimulating and excellent experience and we were assisted a great deal by The Royal Society for the Conservation of Nature. At the end David donated all his father's slides from the original expedition to their custody.

Much more recently David and I decided to repeat this process in southern Spain, in Andalucia's Coto Doñana. This time we would be following in the footsteps of another Guy Mountfort and Eric Hosking book, *Portrait of a Wilderness*. We were to get considerable help from a good friend, Javier Hidalgo, who lives in Sanlúcar de Barrameda on the edge

The author with Paula and Javier Hidalgo at the bodega in Sanlúcar

of the Guadalquivir river. I had first met Javier during my Suffolk days. I was asked by a member of the SWT who owned a wine business whether I could take one of his friends birding. That person turned out to be Javier, whose family business produces perhaps the finest sherry in Spain. His La Gitana Mazanilla is a fine drink and Javier has taught me how to appreciate this tipple as a table wine, particularly with the finest seafood in his local restaurant Casa Bigote.

I had previously stayed with Javier and his wife Paula a couple of times, and David and I were invited to start our visit here. We explored the east side of the river and the coast down as far a Tarifa. We photographed Little Swifts in an old building on the fish market in Chipiona and spent hours on the saltings just north of Sanlúcar, coming face to face with Collared Pratincoles, Greater Flamingos, Red-knobbed Coots and Marbled and White-headed Ducks.

Eventually we moved to the western side of the river, to the Doñana National Park proper, and stayed in the quaint town of El Rocío with its unpaved streets. We were there at the time of the major religious festival when pilgrims from all over Spain assemble. The place was full of people on horseback and with various horse-drawn modes of transport. We were to discover that they did not sleep much either. We visited the various parts of the park which are open to the public. None of these would have been present in the days of Eric Hosking's visits. The cork oaks at the Acebuche centre

revealed wonderful views of Azure-winged Magpies and the
hides reminded me much of their maker. Yes, Bert Axell
played a part in this reserve too.

Azure-winged Magpie is one of the special birds of south-western Spain

We drove out under huge skies to the Valverde centre,
with its enormous colony of nesting waterbirds. Here, in the
most comfortable of situations, you could stand all day and
photograph so many species. There were constant streams of
Glossy Ibises, Cattle and Little Egrets, Purple Herons and
Black-crowned Night-Herons flying backwards and forwards
collecting food for their demanding young. The Glossy Ibises
were particularly interesting as the species is a fairly new

colonist to the area. Their numbers are growing fast and now over 5,000 pairs nest here and the birds are expanding their range all the time. Their urge to take over the world knows no bounds with them reaching the Carmargue recently and each year small groups turning up in the UK. Some birds have even reached Cuba and Trinidad and Tobago. We know this, of course, from colour rings placed on the birds' legs.

Glossy Ibis is now spreading fast in southern Europe and even reaching the UK annually

The great climax of our visit to Doñana, though, was an appointment we had to visit the Palacio, the research station deep within the park. This was where the Mountfort expeditions, of which Eric was a member, had their headquarters. It is so different there today. At the time of the original expeditions in the 1950s there were no roads into the Doñana and everything had to be done on the backs of mules or horses. Today one of the great problems for the area is the main road to the coast on which traffic travels so fast. This traffic presents a great threat for the rare and endangered Iberian Lynx which still clings on here.

The Palacio is a magnificent building and was originally a hunting lodge. It now houses the park staff and a plethora of students studying ecology. It appeared to us that little had changed since the 1950s. Most of the old black-and-white photographs on the walls were in fact those from the expedition, taken by Eric Hosking himself. This was a shock for David and a deeply emotional moment. We were shown around and then had lunch in the same lounge as the three separate expeditions.

After lunch we were taken out and shown the various habitats. We paused by enormous ancient oaks where hundreds of Eurasian Spoonbills and Grey Herons were nesting. The trees looked like they were ready for Christmas with the birds standing in for baubles. These colonies depend on these trees, but in turn the trees could well die back due to the amount of guano deposited on their branches. Continuing we saw Wild Boar and Red Deer and hordes of European Bee-eaters. The highlight was a sighting of a rare Spanish Imperial Eagle hunting over the oaks.

David Hosking (centre) with Francisco and Victor at the Palacio, Coto Doñana, Spain

The experience finished with us attending a reception in Seville where a new book on Doñana was being launched, which included the celebration of the expeditions which made up *Portrait of a Wilderness*. David felt touched to be included in this and we left Doñana much more aware of how the ecology worked and what threats it faced in the future. We will never be able to thank Francisco Ibanez and his colleagues enough for making us so welcome and for taking time to show us such a fantastic place.

We finished that particular trip by driving up to Extremadura to stay with our good friends John and Anthea

Hawkins. We enjoyed a further few days of seeing great birds. Great and Little Bustards, more views of Spanish Imperial Eagles, White-rumped Swifts dashing above Monfragüe Castle and sorting all the larks out on the Bellen plains. Spain is still so good that if I could only go to one place in the world to watch birds then I would go for Spain every time.

We now have to find time to visit the Danube to cover the ground of *Portrait of a River* and we will have completed the revisits of three of those iconic books.

Obviously over the years I had taken every opportunity to travel, mainly in search of birds. My very first adventure abroad was with Beryl in 1968 when we took a package holiday to the Austrian Alps. It was September as this was the only time we could afford, and it was not great for birds. One thing that does stand out was that I saw a lot of Spotted Nutcrackers close to our hotel. This was made all the more interesting by the fact that I had seen one of the Siberian race of this species in Suffolk during that summer.

As the children grew up we satisfied our holiday needs by taking them to Wales and then later became more adventurous and started visiting Scotland. At first we used to visit the Nethy Bridge area, where we could explore the Caledonian Forest and visit Loch Garten for stunning views of Ospreys. We also walked a lot in the woods, finding our own birds. More than once we enjoyed good views of

Western Capercaillie and even came across other Osprey nests when there was only officially one. We took the ski lift to the top of Cairngorm to find Rock Ptarmigan, but later Jeremy and I regularly walked up Carn Ban Mor to come face to face with Eurasian Dotterel. One year we took ringing gear with us and enjoyed ringing our first Crested Tits from our cottage garden.

The kids were urging me to become more adventurous, so one year we booked a caravan on North Uist, in the Outer Hebrides. It took two days to get there but what an exciting adventure it was. Our tiny but perfect caravan was by the sea loch at Caranish. We could go out cockling, bring them back for supper and then play scrabble, which even at a young age Jeremy always won. There were of course birds too. The long-staying Steller's Eider on South Uist was added to our list, but sadly it was in eclipse plumage. The myriad of waders nesting on the machair was impressive and although it was July we did manage to see a couple of Corncrakes.

The weather was wonderful and we had miles of beaches to ourselves. Even the ferry trip back to the mainland was good with huge numbers of Manx Shearwaters on the move, and among them were dozens of Sooty Shearwaters. Minke Whales were also seen, and stopping off on the drive across Skye we enjoyed the harbours full of Common Eiders and Black Guillemots. When the kids returned to school the teacher asked everyone where they had spent their summer holidays. Predictably most kids talked of Mallorca, the Algarve and France, but my own children received puzzled expressions as they spoke gloriously of North Uist.

My children Bronwen and Jeremy at primary school

We had a couple of holidays in France with the children and these, together with the trips to Holland organised through work, persuaded me that I should definitely abandon twitching and go see the birds where they belonged. It was much cheaper to do it this way anyhow. One of our very early holidays with the children was to the Brenne region of France. This area, which really does remind me of East Anglia when I was young, is situated about six hours' drive from Calais and just south of the city of Orléans. It is an area of hundreds of man-made lakes or fish-ponds surrounded by small farms, woodlands and heathlands. This was one of my first real opportunities to be able to see many species that were only rarities in the UK.

The lakes support large populations of Black-necked Grebes and Whiskered Terns, and these were certainly very rare birds in Suffolk. In addition Short-toed Eagles, Black Kites and European Honey-buzzards nested here and the woods held the gigantic Black Woodpecker, Middle Spotted Woodpecker, Hawfinch and Golden Oriole. On the heaths there were Dartford Warblers, Red-backed Shrikes and Cirl Buntings. It was also here that I had my first experience of Little Bustards. Add to that many species of butterflies and dragonflies and wonderful flora, with many orchids. It is still a wonderful place to go and I have visited many more times since.

One of the bonuses of that first trip was to meet Englishman Tony Williams, who at that time was working there for a hunting organisation. That was nearly 30 years ago and Tony is still there and now working for the Ligue pour la Protection des Oiseaux (LPO). He leads walks for visitors taking in all wildlife species and knows everything about that area. He and his wife Michelle and their boys have been great friends for years now and any excuse to visit that area is grabbed eagerly.

I made my first venture across the Atlantic in 1988 with friends Terry Palmer and Peter Newton. Here we visited

Massachusetts and New York State and came face-to-face with many of the species that we had been hoping for on our annual trips to the Isles of Scilly. We also met a number of helpful American birders, many of whom remain friends to this day. One who stands out is my pal Bob Abrams. He is tall and looks like a stretched-out Groucho Marx wearing an enormous bushy moustache. We met on the beach at Plum Island, Massachusetts, in that first year and have been friends ever since. I will never forget his first words "Are you a Limey?" We have met up on many occasions both in the US and in Europe. It was Bob who first introduced me to Cape May Bird Observatory in New Jersey and we have enjoyed many a trip with him and his wife Joan.

My American pal Bob Abrams in a Spanish hide

Through Bob I also met his pal, the gigantic Mike Martinek, who brightened many a trip. His knowledge of British history was superior to that of most people from the UK and he apparently is world-renowned for tying something called fishing flies. Having said that, the skill that I admired most was his amazing ability to identify American wood warblers by their often insect-like songs. It was truly memorable to walk around Mount Auburn Cemetery in Cambridge, Massachusetts, and hear Mike's guttural drawl calling "Butter-butt, Maggie, Black-and-white, Blackburnian" and once "Holy Cow Worm-eating." He is a larger than life character in more ways than one.

It was during those early visits to Massachusetts that I also met Douglas Chickering. Doug is a Plum Island fanatic and keeps meticulous lists of everything he sees. He lives close to this impressive site and spends most of his time birding there. He writes numerous essays on his birding with his partner Lois and nowhere could you read more eloquent accounts of birding at its best. I have been privileged to know all these guys for years now and I am so pleased I was able to show Bob, Joan and Doug birds in Europe as well.

Another great friend from those days was Walter Chapman. He and his then wife Anne took us in when we visited the Adirondacks and then showed us the wildlife of the area. Most memorable was how Chappy followed wood chippings up a small stream to locate the nest of a pair

Willet is a regular bird at Plum Island

of Black-backed Woodpeckers in a small bog. Anne sadly died a year or two later but Chappy, and later his new wife Cathy, met up with me on subsequent trips to the US. Sadly Chappy died in 2012, aged 90, but I am pleased to say he was birding right up until the end.

Chappy lived in a New York State community called Newcomb. This small place was wonderfully situated for wildlife and the people of this area were so welcoming. I returned twice more with birding groups and we were treated so well. Judy Muller lived in a cabin by a wonderful lake known as Beaver Meadow. I remember asking her why 'meadow'? It turned out that the property was a meadow until the Beavers moved in. She demonstrated the effect of Beavers by clearing a dam to let some water off the property, and the Beavers would always have it repaired by the morning. This was a wonderful place where we saw Black Bears and birds like Pileated Woodpecker, Barred Owl, Hooded Merganser and American Black Duck. We were also fortunate to see otters here and once a superb Bobcat.

Great Northern Divers, or Common Loons to give them their local name, are a regular feature of North American boreal lakes

Going back to Cape May, I had read the famous books by Wilbur Stone on the place long before I ever dreamt of visiting. When I did get there I was amazed at how the place had changed since Stone's day. The books were written in the

1930s and it had become so built up during the intervening period. Nevertheless, the impressive migration of birds of prey continues to thrill many people each autumn. I have been there at least seven times and always made to feel welcome at the observatory by the legendary Pete Dunn, together with Marlene Murgatroyd and Sheila Lego who run the engine room of the place. Now my old pal Mike Crewe has crossed the Atlantic to be part of the CMBO team.

A year or two ago my friend Bob Abrams and myself identified and photographed a Common Ground-Dove on Nunney's Island. This was the second record for the state of New Jersey and the first since the 19th century. It was nice to be associated with finding a rarity in the United States.

One of the joys of birding abroad is that you make so many friends. In 1994 my friend David Hosking and I paid a visit to Alaska. We had been invited by Ken and Judy Marlow who live on the Kenai Peninsula. We were put in touch through another naturalist I had met in the Adirondacks, Andy Saunders. Ken and Judy already ran a successful fishing business but wanted to include wildlife tours on their itinerary and wanted to know more about the birds in their area. Hence the invitation.

It was a stunning experience, particularly the boat trips around the peninsula and the opportunity to see and photograph the hordes of seabirds. I shall never forget that first opportunity to be in such spectacular country with thousands of Tufted Puffins hurtling above our heads. We also enjoyed the wonderful views of Sea Otters and other marine mammals. Quietly floating down the Kenai river is another great experience, and it is made even better by Ken's champagne and salmon breakfast on a riverbank. Ken and Judy and their family became great friends and I have ben lucky enough to visit twice more, including a memorable stay with my wife Beryl. The Marlows attended the British Birdwatching Fair at Rutland Water on one occasion so we were able to show them some British birds.

Champagne and salmon breakfast on the Kenai River, Alaska, with Ken Marlow

Another time I visited Alaska to take part in a Wilderness Foundation conference in Anchorage. This was kindly arranged for me by Londoner Toby Aykroyd, who was anxious to set up a European network of large area conservation projects. I spoke at a workshop which was well attended by Europeans but there were no Americans present. I was amazed at the American attitude. The local dignitaries seemed very proud of the destruction they had achieved in their amazing state. In addition, several young delegates who worked for the Government showed me letters they had received upon enrolment telling them they should not get involved in anti-government discussions. Sometimes it is hard to think of the United States as the self-styled 'Land of the Free'.

A Wandering Tattler by an Alaskan stream

Elsewhere in the US we visited Arizona, where we started off our trip at The Grand Canyon. My son Jeremy was with us, and as a geologist he opened my eyes about the origins of this amazing place. We later moved down to the south of the state, staying first in Ramsey Canyon and later in Tucson. We were fortunate to meet relatives of my Suffolk friends David and Claire Barker. The lady of the house, who was well into her eighties, was able to tell stories related by her grandmother of the early pioneering days when she had travelled west by wagon train. The most amazing part of this was how they had lowered their wagons and animals down to the bottom of the Grand Canyon and then hauled them up the other side.

We visited the Sonoran Desert and many more sites as far south as the Mexican border, seeing amazing birds along the way including the likes of Greater Roadrunner and Cactus Wren. Best of all for me, a sad fan of old western films, was a couple of trips to Tombstone. Here you hear the truth about the Gunfight at the OK Corral and wander among the original buildings. I made a point of sitting in Boot Hill Cemetery for an hour until I saw a small bird called a Verdin. The entry from that place in my notebook is still much treasured.

Another time in Arizona we went on a trip to the Organ Pipe Cactus National Monument. We drove west there with Crested Caracara as our target bird. On arrival we had a great time seeing Vermillion Flycatcher, Sora and then eventually the caracara. As we prepared to leave I asked my son for the car keys, which he denied all knowledge of having. He was right because we could both see them on the driver's seat with the

Male Vermilion Flycatcher is a very colourful bird

car safely locked. As we were debating which brick to use to smash a window we spotted a dust cloud getting closer. Soon a vehicle arrived and a small Apache man emerged. We both smiled and shook hands. "You have trouble" he said as we showed him the problem. Then he ran his hand through my ample hair and with an even bigger smile exclaimed "Good job this is not 1894". The penny dropped as this was one of the areas where Geronimo led his band of marauders. My Apache friend called the local police and they soon gained entry to the car and we were on our way again.

Beryl and I first went to Florida in 1989 to celebrate

our silver wedding anniversary. My wife had a remarkable Uncle Kenny who lived in Coral Gables, an area of southern Miami. This gave us a base to explore the Everglades and marvel once again at the extraordinary biodiversity of another of the great wetlands of the world. Despite coastal Florida being so built up, the interior still has so much good bird habitat. We endured terrible biting mosquitoes to come face-to-face with Alligators and great birds like Limpkin, Roseate Spoonbill, Sandhill Crane and much, much more.

We returned a few years later when a friend lent me his house to the south of Orlando. My daughter Bronwen and one of her friends came too. Our accommodation was luxurious with an indoor swimming pool and great access to many wildlife areas. We went on night-time airboat rides looking at Alligators. It was here on one trip that I made a great fool of myself. I had a seen a sign about live interpretation but walked past because I had no idea what it meant. Later we were walking into the site of an old cow camp when a young woman rushed towards me screaming and telling me she had been raped by Indians. I was distraught. I started yelling for help and hoping the Indians were not close by. Only some minutes later did I figure out what was happening. The young woman was an actress and this was live interpretation. Silly me!

I have really enjoyed birding in the USA over the years. Especially away from large urban areas the people are extremely friendly and tolerant and we have enjoyed some great birds in some great places. Only twice have I come across any strange attitudes and this now after over 20 trips on that side of the Atlantic. We are a bit different in the UK in that records from amateur ornithologists make up a huge slice of the data collected for national surveys and studies. Many amateurs involved in ornithology are much more talented than a lot of the professionals and this is widely recognised.

In Arizona we stayed at Ramsey Canyon for a few nights and a friendly young lady in the shop suggested that I should join the staff on their weekly bird census. I turned up at dawn excited at the prospect but was told that I could not accompany them as I was not a professional birder and not able to play a part. The shock of this meant I was unusually speechless and the arrogant chap who passed on this message escaped unscathed.

In Alaska my friend Ken Marlow tried to fix it with the state US Fish & Wildlife Service people to allow me and him to go back into the extreme wilderness forest to look for the scarcer owl species. Again it was intimated that no permits could be given to amateurs. A week or so later, through Ken's son Neil, we found a brood of four young Northern Hawk-owls with parents feeding them on the wild side of Shilak Lake. When we were next in the US Fish & Wildlife Service office we just happened to mention that. When asked where we saw the owls I was very tempted to tell them to get out and find the birds themselves if they were so professional.

These were the only times anywhere in the world where I have come across this attitude.

Brown or Grizzly Bears were something to remember whilst birding in Alaska

We have also ventured further south in the Americas and I have been fortunate to visit Costa Rica on three occasions. This remarkable country has a large proportion of its land area – 19 per cent – protected by nature reserves and national parks. In comparison only 7 per cent of the land area is in similar conservation management in the UK. The biodiversity is high with differing suites of species found on the Pacific and Caribbean slopes, their populations divided by the central spine of mountains. My first encounter with a Resplendent Quetzal will stay with me for a long time. The large number of hummingbird species is another feature of this friendly country.

I saw my first nesting Jabirus in Costa Rica

The birding in Costa Rica can be fast and furious with little time to stop and reflect. I will never forget one of my friends, Adam Gretton, being reduced at tears at the sight of his first Snowcap – a tiny and stunning hummingbird. We only found it at the second attempt, but the very experienced Adam had given up hope when the little jewel appeared right in front of him. And we will never forget the great bonhomie that developed with the locals when we stopped to look at a Black-and-white Owl in their village square. They all knew exactly where the bird was and turned out to ensure all of us on the tour got good views. There are just a few little examples of the joy of birding in this fabulous place.

For anybody wanting to venture to the tropical Americas for some exciting birding then Costa Rica is a must. The country is only the size of Wales but has nearly 900 species. I have now seen over half of these on my three visits. I have friends Paco and Freddy Madrigal and Eric Castro to thank for many of them. It is also such a safe country. Costa Rica feels it has no need for any military forces, just a police force. The people are so friendly and the wildlife fantastic.

The late Lonesome George was a graphic example of how the human race has destroyed our natural world

Thanks are also due to David Hosking for arranging for me to accompany him and a number of wildlife photographers to that Mecca for naturalists, the Galápagos

Islands. Photography has taken up more of my life in recent years, largely thanks to David. Since my back operations ringing has seemed a less attractive option, so it is the camera now which is uppermost when I'm birding. I would not describe myself as a wildlife photographer, more a naturalist who carries a camera.

I digress and should say that with regard to my visit to the Galápagos I have to pinch myself even now to remind myself of that journey. We spent a fortnight on *Cachalote*, a sailing boat which took us around most of the archipelago, enjoying the wildlife that was so influential in Darwin's life and his theories. I found the many species of finches interesting but not dramatic. More up my street were the seabird colonies and being able to walk amongst Red-footed and Nazca Boobies and Great and Magnificent Frigatebirds. Daniel Fitter was our guide and he is an extraordinary chap. His knowledge of the area is second to none and his enthusiasm and leadership were inspirational. I mused as he spoke that his grandfather, Richard Fitter, had been equally inspirational in my life. Another plus for me was the friendship I formed with the Ecuadorian skipper because of our mutual love for the guitarist Carlos Santana. This was a true pilgrimage and stands out as one of my most memorable trips.

More recently I was able to visit the Pantanal in Brazil, which is perhaps the largest wetland in the world. It is also home to the Hyacinth Macaw, one of the most threatened

A wonderful Jaguar resting by a Pantanal river

species of parrot in South America and certainly the biggest. The wetland itself produced many species and an incredible density of birds. I also enjoyed stunning views of mammals like Brazilian Tapir, Giant River Otter and, best of all, Jaguars. Perhaps the most extraordinary experience was sitting out on a terrace after dinner at the Monastery Caraça and watching a splendid Maned Wolf come for its supper.

Brazil is an impressive country and so big. There has been a lot of habitat destruction but vast areas like the Pantanal still exist. There is a particularly good example of ecotourism at work in this area. Hyacinth Macaw is still a rare bird but at one time its population was as low as 200 pairs. Local ranchers realised that lots of people wanted to visit the Pantanal to see this bird. These ranchers set up lodges to house visitors and erected large nest boxes for the macaws. The outcome is that over 2,000 pairs of this gorgeous bird can now be found in this area.

Hyacinth Macaw is the biggest parrot in the world

The wetland birds of the Pantanal are very impressive. This must be one of the best places in the world to see the enormous Jabiru stork. Flocks of this great bird feed in the ponds by the Transpantaneira highway, along with equally bountiful numbers of Wood Storks and Roseate Spoonbills. A number of heron species can be found, but the large groups of

The Great Potoo demonstrates the art of camouflage at its best

Capybaras and Caiman are what really catch the eye.

Late evening boat trips were also memorable. Cruising along in motor boats we could feel the millions of insects hitting our faces. As dusk fell the sky was full of Nacunda Nighthawks and Bulldog Bats taking advantage of the emerging feast. On occasions we also caught glimpses of the enormous, owl-like Great Potoos cruising through the sky and hoovering up their supper.

My African travels have taken me to Gambia and Morocco, but most memorably to Kenya, which was another trip with the Hosking family. Here all the images of many TV programmes became reality. We enjoyed the wilderness

African Rock Python devouring a Great White Pelican at Lake Nakuru, Kenya

of the Masai Mara, the Rift Valley sites like Lake Naivasha, Lake Nakuru and Lake Baringo, and finished up in the beautiful, rugged Samburu National Reserve. Coming so close to the large mammals was amazing. It brought alive the many images from those old natural history films from TV. Perhaps my greatest memory was watching an African Rock Python consume a Great White Pelican. We sat patiently photographing the grisly spectacle and wondering what all the other birds standing around would do. The digestion lasted for over four hours and we watched the lot. We never did see the reaction of the other birds as they were frightened off by another jeep which approached and drove right in front of us. I was furious but did retreat when I noticed that the newcomer was Joanna Lumley and a film crew. Our driver, Uticus, was delighted when the whole thing was over as he had sweated profusely for the whole time. He later confessed to being terrified of these huge snakes.

African Elephants on the move in Samburu

More recently I have enjoyed a couple of visits to India. This included Ranthambore for Tigers and lots of birds. We had to work hard for our Tiger but on our last drive we were successful in seeing a pair. We owe a huge amount to our driver, Amin Khan, who took so much trouble to make sure we had good views and got great photographs. We moved on to Bharatpur, the Chambal River and Agra for the Taj Mahal. Bharatpur was very dry but still an exciting place to be. The

Chambal River was very special, not only for the rare Indian Skimmers, but also the prehistoric looking Gharials and the Ganges River Dolphin. I tolerated Agra but the poverty and squalor took away some the grandeur of the Taj Mahal.

The prehistoric looking Gharial is numerous on the Chambal River

We moved up to the Himalayan foothills as far as Pangot, where the diversity of birds was terrific. New species came so quickly that I could not cope with the brief views of everything that was being pointed out. I swear that Golden Bush Robin, Siberian Rubythroat and Himalayan Rubythroat were all added to my list in less than a minute. The air was cold and crisp and the birding good. The early morning views of the highest Himalayan peaks were awe-inspiring and it was only when looking at them that I realised how high we were. I was to suffer with severe altitude sickness before we descended to our next destination. We were to end this trip at the legendary Corbett National Park. When visiting the Isles of Scilly in the 1970s I had got to know David Hunt quite well. Visiting Corbett was therefore a bit nostalgic as this was where David was killed by a Tiger whilst leading a birding trip in 1985.

Bengal Tiger – coming so close to such a mammal was truly thrilling

Corbett was also an exciting place for wildlife, even if a night at the Government Guest House at Dhikala was a dire experience. My own room had no working electric light bulbs, while other people had various forms of wildlife in their rooms. This was more than compensated for by the wonderful birds and mammals. Seeing Asian Elephants was a great thrill, while the memorable birds included the likes of Brown and Tawny Fish-Owls and Pallas's Fish-Eagle, while even some of the more subtle species like Puff-throated Babbler have lived long in the memory.

Outside the park there was some more good birding. The River Kosi was a must for early morning visits with many wetland birds, but the main target was the enigmatic Ibisbill. This site is also one of the best places in the world to watch Wallcreepers in winter as they descend to feed among the large boulders on the river bed. All around this area we saw so much, and always in the company of wonderful people.

I went back to India the following year, 2011, but this time to lead a trip for Indian Wildlife Tours, taking participants to see a combination of wildlife and World Cup cricket. We visited the Tadoba National Park where we enjoyed views of Tiger, Gaur, Sloth Bear and many birds. The second site was the Sundarbans in the Bay of Bengal. This enormous wetland was very impressive with so much to see, but a major memory was staying in a local village with local people looking after us. Cruising around all day through large tracts of mangroves we saw lots of wetland birds. Kingfishers were numerous, with the large Brown-winged Kingfisher being the most spectacular. We were amused too by the Red Junglefowl. We could not get used to seeing what amounted to a chicken get up and hurtle over the treetops.

Shorebirds were spectacular, and in particular the large numbers of Terek Sandpipers seen.

The cricket was good too. At Nagpur we saw Australia beat New Zealand whilst a Black-shouldered Kite hovered over the pitch and Dusky Crag Martins nested in the stands. At Bangalore we witnessed an incredible tie between India and England in front of a huge noisy crowd. Strauss and Tendulkar both scored centuries. When the floodlights came on Black Kites picked up flying insects whilst the game went on regardless.

The White-breasted Kingfisher is very common in India

I have already mentioned that my son Jeremy is employed by Shell, and over the years he has worked in some interesting places. After leaving Holland he first spent seven years living near Muscat in Oman. We were able to visit the family there on five occasions. This was a fantastic opportunity to get to grips with the birds of the Arabian Peninsula. I had already grown to love desert birding in Jordan and these visits further whetted my appetite. Oman is a large country and most of my birding was confined to the north. I was lucky to meet Jens and Hanne Eriksen, two of the best wildlife photographers on earth, who lived in the country and whose knowledge of its birds is second to none. They helped me to see many exciting species and I remember one splendid evening watching first Lichtenstein's Sandgrouse coming to drink followed by a flypast of Egyptian Nightjars in the gathering gloom.

A visit to the Sunub rubbish tip was also a must in those days. If you could put up with the stench you could enjoy the sight of dozens of eagles and vultures coming to the offal dump. Steppe Eagles formed the bulk of the gathering, but Eastern Imperial and Greater Spotted Eagles were also there. Egyptian Vultures and enormous Lappet-faced Vultures made up the remainder of this impressive throng of raptors. We had some wonderful experiences in Oman, not least visiting a beach at night to see Green Turtles laying their eggs. We ventured to Salalah in the south where the avifauna is more African, whereas in the north it is mainly Indian. We walked amongst frankincense trees and watched great rafts of Socotra Cormorants offshore.

My wife Beryl birding Omani style

The people in Oman were also remarkably friendly and helpful. Beryl and I felt perfectly safe driving around in the desert and stopping anywhere to watch birds or to have a picnic. On one occasion we were well down the coast south of Quriyat, watching birds by some lagoons and enjoying our lunch containing fruits we had purchased in the local markets. Suddenly distant dust turned into a vehicle heading our way. We were a little nervous as it kept coming directly to us and finally stopped alongside. Out stepped two bearded locals covered in dust and sand. They politely enquired whether we were okay. Did we have gas? Did we have water? Was the vehicle okay? They were simply concerned because vehicles do not normally hang around in that place unless they have broken down and they were just checking. I guess they do not see that many British birders, but their concern was much appreciated.

The lofty mountain village of Bilad Sayt in Oman is home to Lappet-faced Vultures

We drove along stony wadis up into the mountains above Niswah. Here we visited the amazing terraced village of Bilad Sayt and strolled amongst the almond blossom looking for Hume's and Hooded Wheatears. We ventured south along the coast to Quriyat, marvelling at the huge flocks of Great Black-headed and Sooty Gulls. Oman still beckons me back and I must try and visit again before too long.

Jeremy then moved on to a posting in Brunei on the island of Borneo. We only managed to go once to this paradise but it was a memorable visit. The house was set in a beautiful area with tall forest patches and open grassland with storm ditches. Birding in the garden was very satisfying. A flock of over 40 Oriental Pied Hornbills came to roost each evening and a Malayan Night-Heron hunted the ditches. Scarlet Sunbirds fed on the blooms in the garden and Collared Kingfishers kept up a noisy presence.

Birding in Brunei with my son Jeremy

Visits to coastal lagoons produced a few birds and Grey-tailed Tattler was added to my list. The forests were full of noises early in the morning. Gibbons began the chorus followed by birds such as Rhinoceros and Wreathed Hornbills. One morning we had a brief and tantalising view of a pair of the endemic Bornean Bristlehead in a dead tree, but an evening flight of 700 fruit-bats was equally exciting. We also enjoyed a river trip to see a group of Proboscis Monkeys.

Whilst in Brunei we took out two weeks to go with the family to Western Australia. This was a wonderful surprise and for the first week we stayed in a cottage by the impressive Karri Forest. Sitting in a hot tub with a gin and tonic listening to Southern Boobok owls was a new experience. The area was

The Laughing Kookaburra is a common and noisy bird throughout much of Australia

spectacular and every morning kangaroos and Emus grazed the meadow by the cottage and a pair of Wedge-tailed Eagles passed by overhead. We explored the forest, enjoying the hordes of Australian Ringneck and Western Rosella parrots. The second part of the trip was spent in Perth. There was much to explore here too. Herdsman Lake was a favourite place. Surrounded by urban development, this huge wetland was a haven for Yellow-billed Spoonbill, Straw-necked and Australian White Ibises and many wildfowl including the weird Musk Duck. Nearby Lake Monger was similar but muddier and therefore had good numbers of Red-necked Avocets.

Australian Ringnecks, or '28s', are a common sight in Western Australia

For the last three years Jeremy has been based in Calgary in Canada, and this is where he and his family are planning to settle as he has applied for residency. The city is within an hour of the Rocky Mountains and bordered to the east and south by extensive prairies and their accompanying wetlands.

It is a perfect place to be. Calgary is a very green city with numerous parks and reserves, and the green corridor of the Bow River runs through the area.

The mountains are spectacular at any season and we have had one winter and two summer visits so far. The wild flowers in summer are spectacular and the mammals so exciting. We have had great views of Grizzly and Black Bears, Mountain Goats, Bighorn Sheep, Elk, Moose, Timber Wolf and many more. The birds are also plentiful with Barrow's Goldeneye, Harlequin Duck and Bufflehead on most rivers and lakes and woodpeckers galore in the forests, as well as Pine Grosbeaks – another must-see species for European birders. At one special place I have been fortunate to watch the enigmatic Great Grey Owl at very close quarters.

The prairies have many wetlands and Frank Lake remains one of my favourite places. In early summer the place is full of wildfowl. Huge numbers of species such as Redhead, Canvasback, Lesser Scaup, Ruddy Duck and Northern Pintail occur. Rafts of Black-necked Grebes and smaller numbers of Western Grebes also occupy the water. Shorebirds can be exciting with Black-necked Stilt, American Avocet, Marbled Godwit, Willet and Short-billed Dowitcher all present. A colony of White-faced Ibis and thousands of Franklin's and a smaller number of California Gulls nest. The highlight for me, though, are the large flocks of Wilson's Phalaropes, many of which stay to breed.

Being so close to a Great Grey Owl was one of the great birding moments of my life

During the winter snows we spent a day in the frozen prairies and were rewarded with huge flocks of Common Redpolls which held a few Arctic Redpolls, but best of all was finding several gorgeous Snowy Owls. The partly frozen rivers in Calgary were worth checking out with flocks of Common Goldeneye, Mallard and Bufflehead being constantly harassed by Bald Eagles. The forests around the town abounded with large flocks of Bohemian Waxwings and smaller numbers of Pine Grosbeaks. In temperatures permanently below freezing I was astonished at how many birds were present.

On one of our Calgary trips we stopped off at Toronto to visit relatives in rural Ontario. It was an interesting

This Snowy Owl was spending the winter on the frozen Alberta prairies

experience. This was much more of an agricultural area and I have to say that the residents were not particularly friendly. I walked the lanes with my camera and whilst photographing a sign on a farm gate received a very hostile reception. The sign stated that the farm was part of a wildlife friendly farming syndicate and I was immediately interested. The female farmer greeted my questions with indifference and basically told me to mind my own business and push off.

The birds were very different on this side of the country and I was finding the eastern counterparts of many of the species we had seen in Calgary, for example Eastern Bluebirds instead of Mountain Bluebirds. The agricultural fields were full of breeding Killdeers, a wonderful noisy plover. Black-

and-yellow Bobolinks were everywhere, hanging above the grassland and emitting their bell-like calls.

As we drove around the fairly bland landscape I discovered a large conservation area with promising habitats. I later found out that this was a project creating wildlife corridors between the Great Lakes and the boreal north. This was a paradise for me and I spent two days wandering these areas on my own. It was here that I discovered how useless I was on North American birdsong without some local assistance. Ovenbirds with their 'Teacher, teacher, teacher' songs were everywhere but I never set eyes on one. I did manage to find several beautiful male Indigo Buntings perched up in full song, but the various trills of the wood warblers tested me thoroughly, especially as I could not see the birds most of the time. I needed Mike Martinek, my friend from Boston, Massachusetts, more than I realised.

I did manage to find Pine, Chestnut-sided and Black-and-white Warblers. Other birds included Great Crested Flycatcher, Wood Thrush, Red-tailed Hawk, Northern Cardinal, Belted Kingfisher and a plethora of sparrows of which most seemed to be Song or Swamp. We also managed two days in Algonquin National Park. This was more like the Rockies with large tracts of boreal habitat. Here we had more chances to look at Moose but failed to find any bears. More birds obliged, though, and we added Northern Parula, Magnolia Warbler and Purple Finch to our list.

With a little effort a photo of Niagara Falls can be made to look wild and remote

Thanks to the endurance of our hosts Margaret and Leslie we also managed to spend a day at Niagara Falls. This was one of the biggest shocks of my life. I have this theory that whatever the wonders you see on TV they are always a bit of a disappointment when you see the real thing. For instance when I visited Kenya I assumed the whole countryside was full of big game. I was quite miffed to find I would have to drive through thousands of acres of agricultural land before I saw a single zebra. Well Niagara was very similar. I never realised that there was so much urban development alongside the spectacular falls. Nor did I realise how trashy it all was. Imagine multiplying Great Yarmouth seafront by 20 and then you get the idea. However, just like the TV cameramen I always found ways of making my photographs look wild and remote.

Perhaps the most bizarre of my travels was a visit to Russia. It was in 1991, just as Gorbachev handed over power to Yeltsin. The Suffolk Wildlife Trust education staff had been involved in a project with the Environment Agency, The Broads Authority and the University of Hertfordshire. The project involved carrying out research on a river system and setting up an education centre for children around a village called Polishi. Polishi is south of the city of Vladimir, which is about 120 miles east of Moscow. Money had been given to the area by the British Council and project members were concerned that this cash was not being used effectively. So with others I visited the area to try and get things moving and therefore ease the concerns of the funding body.

I flew on my own to Moscow and expected to find somebody holding up a board with my name on it. I could find nobody until a young man approached me clutching a page from the SWT magazine which contained my photograph. He led me outside to where a group of men were standing by a large but old black car. I quickly discovered that protocol in Russia demands that a guest is welcomed by somebody of equal rank. No regional NGOs existed in Russia in those days so the Chairman of the local environment committee was my host. We boarded the large car and set off out onto a motorway.

After about an hour there was a very loud clanking noise from underneath the car and we ground to a halt. The driveshaft had fractured and was lying on the ground under the car, which was now positioned on the hard shoulder. It was then that I discovered another important challenge for Russians at that time. They had obviously not been required to make any decisions under the Communist regime so they all stood around staring at the problem and doing nothing. I was tired and it was beginning to rain. My requests to get another vehicle or get me to a hotel until something could be done were always met with the same retort "Not possible".

After another hour of nothing happening I decided to flag down a car and see if we could get a lift. This made the young man who was obviously my minder very uncomfortable. Eventually I found a chap who was very keen on my offer of US$100 (which was equivalent at the time to three months' salary) to get us to our destination. He only had a small Lada so we had to leave our driver and another person behind while the rest of us piled into the cramped car and off we went.

After another hour it was obvious that we had a puncture. Not a problem I thought, but to my horror the driver had no spare wheel. We limped to a farm, where to my amazement a wheel was quickly found and we were off again within half an hour. The driver was obviously keen to establish himself in

Formula One. He was going flat out on a two-lane highway, but driving straight down the middle and weaving in and out between large lorries. It was not surprising that very soon I had to pay US$20 for a speeding ticket. Eventually, to my horror, we got another puncture. With no hope of another spare wheel, and being only a mile or so from our destination, I paid off the hapless driver and walked to my accommodation.

If you think the situation could not get worse you are very wrong. From what I could gather I was to be staying at an old communist sanatorium for sick workers. The plan was to meet here with others and we would head on to Polishi. My room was incredibly basic and my excitement at the prospect of a shower was entirely misplaced as it did not work. Entering a communal shower I was so embarrassed to find women and children showering in close proximity that I was out of there lightning fast.

We eventually arrived in Polishi, where my accommodation was in a large, modern, wooden house where I was to sleep on what was effectively a balcony. The heads of the household were very influential people and the man of the house often seemed to have a revolver in his pocket. Every supper time was a huge challenge – exactly how big a challenge depended on the number of men present. Every man would speak at length and propose a toast which was taken with homemade vodka and a pickled cucumber. By the third evening I was so intoxicated that I could hardly walk. The solution was to retire to the sauna and pour gallons of freezing cold water over my head. It did work.

It was whilst sitting quietly on a bench in the village square that another strange event occurred. An elderly local man approached and in perfect English asked me if I knew Great Yarmouth. I was taken aback. I enquired how he knew of the place and discovered that he was a crew member on timber boats which delivered wood to Jewsons, and he regularly visited there before he retired. I didn't dare ask if he knew Michael Seago.

Polishi was a weird village. It was surrounded by vast peat marshes and bogs. My visit was in September, so not the best time of year for the chance of finding good birds. There were

Eurasian Crane – one of the few birds of note seen on Polishi's smouldering peatlands

lots of Common Cranes in the area and also a few Whiskered and White-winged Terns. The most memorable thing was that large areas of peat seemed to be permanently on fire. This produced a strange atmosphere and the feeling of being on another planet. The community was very fond of its magnificent church, a building which people were forbidden from entering during communist rule. They told stories of anyone who disobeyed this instruction being whisked away and not seen again. They insisted that every village had a communist informer. What a dreadful life it must have been.

Before returning to the UK I was taken on a journey to see the amazing town of Suzdal. I had never heard of this place but the memories still pervade of a settlement which is made up entirely of medieval buildings. There are many churches and monasteries as well as fortifications. It is a wonderful and impressive place and well worth visiting. It was the highlight of my visit to Russia.

When we got down to business we were persuaded that all was well with how the money from the grant was being spent. After being in two more vehicles which broke down, including one that failed to cross a ford and floated off downriver, I finally returned to the UK grateful that my Russian travelling experience was at an end.

7.

Retirement of a Sort

Once I retired I looked forward to continuing my interest in birds and nature conservation. I was not prepared for what happened next. My old Trust in Suffolk kindly made Beryl and I Honorary Life Members, and to this day Chief Executive Julian Roughton has been so kind in keeping me in the loop about the development of the organisation. The same cannot be said for other Wildlife Trusts. The rest of the movement appeared to shut the door on me by the Monday following my departure. It was made quite clear that once I had gone they did not require any further involvement from me, although this was never said up front. My work in the Trusts had lasted more than 40 years as a volunteer and then a staff member, and to this day I remain slightly bitter and sad that I am no longer encouraged to play any part in their activities. Retiring from a crusade is not the same as leaving an ordinary job. I am not pretending that I am an easy person to work with. I am passionate about nature conservation and I am always trying to find new ways to improve its position. In addition I cannot tolerate others who do not offer a similar commitment. One leading national figure in The Wildlife Trusts went as far as saying that they needed a rest from my type of person. "We cannot cope with anybody with so many ideas and extreme views – we need a rest from that for a while," was his response to my offer of help.

I was not alone. David Erwin, who had become a like-minded friend, also retired as Chief Executive of the Ulster Wildlife Trust at about the same time as me. He too received the cold shoulder after being in the post for some time, and previous to that acting as a trustee and Chairman. He and I have stayed in touch, together with Steve Sankey, the former Director of the Scottish Wildlife Trust. In later years the three of us came to be known as 'The Celtic Fringe'. It does seem a shame to let all that experience go to waste.

I have found other places to focus my energies. I was Chairman of the Farming and Wildlife Advisory Group (FWAG) in Wales for a while and helped to get them moving before the National FWAG charity became bankrupt in

2011. I am delighted that FWAG has emerged again in Wales and continues to encourage farmers in nature conservation.

I am currently Chairman of the Welsh Ornithological Society and have worked hard with my fellow trustees to give the society a place in Wales, co-ordinating and representing the Welsh bird clubs and societies. I have also just joined the RSPB Advisory Committee for Wales, so my conservation and bird interest is sated by that involvement.

The declining Northern Lapwing thrives at Elmley because of a management regime introduced by the owner and manager

More recently Philip Merricks asked me to join the Management Committee of the Elmley National Nature

Reserve in Kent. This is an enormous wetland site and a fantastic place for breeding waders and wildfowl. It has one of the most impressive breeding populations of Northern Lapwings remaining in southern Britain and its success is largely down to the work of Philip, who owns the land, together with his manager Steve Gordon. Philip is a great example of a farmer who has become infatuated with the wildlife on his land and he is leading the way in making sure that it is well looked after. I am so very happy to be part of that.

Beryl and I have settled into life in Wales rather well. In those early days I had an office near Bridgend and another in Cardigan. There was a journey of over 100 miles between the two. We found a suitable home in the village of Salem, which is snuggled in the hills just to the north of Llandeilo in Carmarthenshire. The house is roughly equidistant between the two offices, and it is close to the splendid Tywi Valley, which is rich in wildlife and to an extent satisfies my need to watch birds. In summer the valley is home to nesting Little Ringed Plover, Common Sandpiper, Goosander and thousands of Sand Martins. The wet woods have a small population of Lesser Spotted Woodpecker, while Common Buzzard, Red Kite, Northern Goshawk, Eurasian Hobby and Peregrine Falcon soar overhead. The woods on the valley slopes have Pied Flycatcher, Common Redstart and a few Wood Warblers. The valley also has a very good population of otter, but you have to be very patient to catch a glimpse of one of these supreme fish-catchers.

The one negative side to the valley is its lack of easy access. Roads do cross the valley at Cilsan and Dryslwyn, but there is no riverside access and this is discouraged anyway by the people who own the fishing rights. I always thought that fishermen may own the fishing rights but not necessarily the land. Their garish and tasteless signs, challenging anyone to enter, adorn too many places in the valley. This is such a great shame as there is a disused railway line running between Llandeilo and Carmarthen and this would make an ideal path, which could be opened up without disturbing the interests of anyone. There is a recently formed Tywi Rivers Trust but I see no signs of any access improvement.

Red Kites are now an almost daily sight in Wales

I have had amazing luck in the Tywi Valley. Friend Julian Friese was living down on the valley floor when, on 6th November 2005, there were serious floods. Julian called just before midday to say that he was watching a gull on the flooded fields which had a very dark mantle. His description seemed to fit that of Laughing Gull, a rarity from the eastern seaboard of the United States. I rushed out, telling Beryl that I would be back shortly. She did not believe that of course. On arrival at Julian's cottage I was horrified at how high the water-level was getting, but with wellington boots on we waded across the yard and there on a small grass island was indeed a first-winter Laughing Gull. I was very pleased as I had not seen the species before in the UK, although I had encountered it many times in the United States. We immediately started telephoning various Carmarthen birders to let them know.

After a few minutes the bird flew off and sadly we could not relocate it. Luckily, when looking at the bird my old fashioned disciplines kicked in and I wrote a brief description of what I could see on a scrap of paper. That was to come in handy a little later. By now birders Barry and Sandra Stewart and Rob Hunt had appeared, and they looked pretty fed up that the bird had gone. We kept scanning around in case it was still present, but the water was continuing to rise and most of the grass islands had gone. Suddenly I realised that a few Black-headed Gulls had flown on to one of the islands and that there was a dark-mantled gull with them. It's back, I thought, so I called the others over. As soon as I focused the telescope on the bird I noticed that it had a very prominent whitish eye-ring, a dusky nape and a short bill. This did not fit my description of the bird seen only 20 minutes previously. I knew what it was and Barry and I both shouted "Franklin's Gull" at the same moment.

This species is much rarer even than Laughing Gull, and I had only ever seen one once before, as a vagrant in Suffolk. Franklin's Gulls breed much further west in the prairie regions of the western United States and Canada. Now I was confused. Had I made a mistake with the first bird? My notes suggested that there might be two very rare birds present, and of two different species. Surely this was too much of a coincidence? Barry and Sandra had digiscoped the Franklin's Gull, so they suggested that they should go to check the area around Dryslwyn Bridge while the rest of us would remain at this site.

You imagine my relief when a little later Barry called me on my mobile to tell me that he was watching a first-winter Laughing Gull. We were all delighted. It does illustrate, though, just how important it is to write down a few notes when looking at a rare or scarce bird, especially if you cannot get a decent photograph. When I finally got into my car to head home for lunch I realised that it was nearly 4pm. You see what birding can do to you. I was so immersed that I had forgotten about eating. People who know me well will find that impossible to believe.

Living in Mid Wales I have many opportunities to visit old haunts. Tregaron Bog is only a short drive through the dramatic Cambrian Hills and the RSPB's superb Gwenffrwd-Dinas reserve is even closer. The latter site is fantastic, with high densities of breeding Pied Flycatcher, Wood Warbler and Common Redstart. Tree Pipit, Whinchat, European Stonechat and Northern Wheatear nest on the surrounding hills and Grey Wagtail, White-throated Dipper and Goosander alongside the rushing streams. It is the perfect Welsh site.

The classic shot of a Puffin with a bill full of sand eels

Our house is only just over an hour away from Pembrokeshire, so I still enjoy an annual visit to Skomer. It is worth the effort just to meet up with the boatmen, Kenny and Carl, but as soon as I am on the island I can sink myself into the smells and noises of its immense seabird colonies. I never tire of watching the Atlantic Puffins and have more photographs of them than I really need. It is so nice to walk amongst the pink thrift, bluebells and pink campion, through colonies of noisy gulls, until the nasal calls of Red-billed Choughs catch my attention. This makes me stop and consider how fortunate we are that conservation has allowed this paradise to survive. The Skomer experience can be enhanced by staying overnight and sharing the darkness with thousands of Manx Shearwaters and maybe a few European Storm-petrels. For the more adventurous you might like to spend a few days on the neighbouring island of Skokholm.

If you include Grassholm, with its 70,000 plus Northern Gannets, and Ramsey, which is now rid of its rats, this archipelago deserves maximum nature conservation attention. It is as good an experience as I have enjoyed anywhere in the world. I have also been fortunate to accompany Cliff Benson of the Sea Trust on a few occasions, on his many marine forays to monitor cetaceans and other wildlife. These trips are truly exciting. Once we were surrounded by hundreds of Common Dolphins, which were turning the surface of the ocean into white water. On another memorable day we sailed into a pod of at least a dozen gigantic Fin Whales. Here we watched their interaction with hundreds of Manx Shearwaters, with the latter taking advantage of the food disturbed by the great mammals.

There are many other superb sites in Pembrokeshire. Fishguard is another of my favourite areas, and especially watching for seabirds at nearby Strumble Head. Work here, pioneered by the likes of Graham Rees, the late Jack Donovan and the late Stuart Devonald, has shown that enormous numbers of seabirds funnel into the Irish Sea, particularly after strong gale-force winds. Graham reminds me, though, that any day has the potential to be productive, for example on 23rd August 2005 when a Sooty Tern flew past Strumble in flat calm conditions. I have been particularly lucky on my visits there. I have seen all four skua species in one morning on more than one occasion. And I saw my only Wilson's Storm-petrel there thanks again to considerable help from Graham.

Then there is Carmarthenshire itself, with the wonderful Burry Inlet just a half an hour away from home. In winter huge ensembles of waders and wildfowl frequent the estuary, with Eurasian Oystercatcher being the most numerous species. Carmarthen Bay is home to over 20,000 Common Scoter in winter and careful scrutiny often reveals a vagrant Surf Scoter from North America among them. When I

Baird's Sandpiper – a rare visitor from America to a Pembrokeshire beach

arrived in Carmarthenshire local birders were trying to set
up a county bird club, and also to get the production of their
annual county bird report in better order. I was asked to join
in and became the first Chairman of the Carmarthenshire
Bird Club, and I also took on the job of doing the bird
report for two or three years. This enabled me to meet
many local birders and form new friendships. John Lloyd
was particularly helpful and it was he who first took me
along to a Welsh Ornithological Society meeting. Wendell
Thomas is the backbone of the bird club and he ensures that
its members meet up regularly both indoors and on field
trips. He provides everything that is essential in any such

organisation and deserves enormous credit for his efforts. Julian Friese has done much to introduce me to local birding spots and Barry and Sandra Stewart have enticed me into Glamorgan and particularly to the Gower, and even once to India.

The author with Welsh birders celebrating a Glaucous-winged Gull in Carmarthenshire

Working with the Welsh Ornithological Society has also been extremely satisfying. After a small period of time spent reorganising the structure, the Council has achieved wonders in repositioning the society so that it is in the relevant position of co-ordinating all of the work of the bird clubs, societies and groups on an all-Wales basis. This is very important when presenting opinions to the Welsh Assembly on matters which affect our birds.

Having persuaded the iconic Welsh TV birder Iolo Williams to become our President we have also improved our publications and rectified what was a precarious financial situation. We run an annual conference which is held at various venues around Wales and this is now a sell-out on each occasion. Any surplus from these events is ploughed back into funding small grants to help research carried out on birds in the principality. I have thoroughly enjoyed being involved, and as an Englishman I appreciate being made to feel so welcome by so many people.

My void after retirement has been largely filled by another project far from the shores of the UK. In 2000 my son Jeremy called to say that he had bought a vineyard. After initial visions of producing a family wine had disappeared he explained that it was a defunct vine field of about three acres. He suggested that I purchase a smaller field next to it. The idea was to build a house here. Jeremy was working for Shell and being sent all over the world, and he wanted a European base to share with his Dutch wife Saskia and their three children.

We followed Jeremy's advice and bought the field, and after I retired we set about creating a French home on this idyllic spot known as Montcélèbre. Anybody who has read Peter Mayall's book *A Year in Provence* will be well aware of the difficulties in doing anything in rural France, but by

Les Hirondelles – our French house

2007 we had achieved our dream and we had our house, Jeremy and Saskia had theirs, and Saskia's father Henk had one too, all amidst this small hillside community on the southern slope of the Cévennes. What's more the houses were completed only one year behind schedule.

Just a year prior to Jeremy coming up with this idea I had been in a small artist's town called Collioure, just to the south of Perpignan. I delivered a talk for a Eurosite AGM on the importance of using rare local breeds of livestock in conservation grazing. The event was held in the very pretentious castle overlooking the harbour and I was so impressed with the area. It was November and the snowy Pyrénéan peak of Canigou towered over us.

We took an excursion over the border into Spain to visit the nature reserve at Aiguamolls de l'Empordà, adjacent to the Gulf of Roses. I was eager to see the place because it was yet another connection with the ubiquitous Bert Axell. I was delighted to meet Jordi Sargatal, who is the man most responsible for the creation of this wetland. Back in 1976 all of this land was threatened by urban development and the young Jordi was on a mission. His quest was to get the local authority to protect the land permanently and create what is there today. This young man's determination won the day and, believe it or not, Jordi made his way to Minsmere to enlist Bert to help create the reserve. Bert obliged and there is a slight hint of Minsmere about the place.

After my few days in Collioure I was already in love with the place. It was an easy decision to buy the land and build the house, knowing that we would be only just over an hour away from Collioure and just two hours from that Spanish wetland. Both are now visited regularly.

For Beryl and I a completely new chapter in our lives was about to begin. I could once again return to being a naturalist and birder on my little patch of land. Its position at the southern tip of the Haut-Languedoc natural park meant that it was rich in wildlife and enjoyed many similarities to Suffolk in the days when I was a child. I had found a sort of paradise.

We have spent up to five months a year at our French

Hoopoes are a feature of our French garden in spring and summer

home and I have made many new friends, including quite a few who share my enthusiasm for birds and wildlife. The area itself is outstanding. Our house is surrounded by garrigue scrubland and a series of large gorges. The ancient Cathar village of Minerve is just a kilometre or two away.

For birds the area is unbeatable. From our garden we have seen a number of raptor species. Montagu's Harrier, Short-toed Eagle and Common Kestrel all breed in the area and are regularly seen from the house during summer. Golden Eagles also breed locally and are occasionally seen. Griffon Vultures commuting between the Tarn Gorges and the Pyrénées are often picked up high in the sky and huge numbers of European Honey-buzzards can pass overhead during migration times. Add to these Eurasian Sparrowhawk, Northern Goshawk, Eurasian Hobby, Peregrine Falcon, Hen Harrier, Common Buzzard, Booted Eagle, Osprey and Black and Red Kites and you can see the level of diversity that occurs.

Sardinian, Subalpine, Melodious and Western Orphean Warblers nest nearby, Hoopoe and Red-rumped Swallow occur around the property, and only last year a pair of Woodchat Shrikes reared a brood in the bushes alongside our garden. European Bee-eaters migrate overhead in large numbers and a pair or two of glorious European Rollers nest close by. Eurasian Scops Owls nest in our hedge and Eurasian Eagle Owls can occasionally be heard calling. My garden bird list currently stands at 121 species.

Two-tailed Pasha butterflies come to our French garden in late summer to feed on figs

Now I have more time I have been able to concentrate on some of the other creatures which occur in our garden. Both Natterjack Toads and Stripeless Tree Frogs call on balmy summer nights, and during the day we often see huge Ocellated Lizards on our property. Butterflies are spectacular and I already have a species list which might make my garden an SSSI back in the UK. The spectacular Swallowtail, Scarce Swallowtail, Cleopatra, Great Banded Grayling and Southern White Admiral are the most obvious, but there are many others. A favourite is the dashing Two-tailed Pasha, which is mainly seen in late summer as it comes to feed on ripening figs. The lavender plants attract hordes of smaller insects including large numbers of Hummingbird Hawkmoths. One of the most striking insects, though, is the Giant Peacock Moth.

Hummingbird Hawkmoths are common in our French garden

The flora is impressive too, and the fringes of the garden have Pyramidal, Lady, Yellow Bee and Early Spider Orchids. Later asphodels abound and the pink colour of Wild Gladioli is striking. The scent of wild thyme exudes at every step.

Our paradise is just a couple of hours from the Pyrénées, where it is possible to watch Lammergeier, Alpine Chough, Rufous-tailed Rock Thrush and many other exciting species. We are also just a couple of hours from the Massif Central with its Griffon and Black Vultures, and the same distance from the Camargue and all that it has to offer. The Mediterranean coast is less than an hour away.

As I mentioned I have made many friends there too, including Ron and Jane Bennett from Autignac. Ron was probably the first birder I got to know and the manner of our introduction was amazing. I was watching raptors at Snickers Gap in Virginia, USA, when a car with a Welsh flag on it caught my eye. The vehicle was owned by Barbara and John Perry from Washington D.C., and after chatting for a while they announced that they had just been staying in France with a Ron Bennett who would be keen to meet me. Well we did meet and we have enjoyed a lot of birding together. We have often been accompanied by John Andrews, and more recently by Paul Williams. I joined the local group of the Ligue pour la Protection des Oiseaux (LPO) and soon met up with Canadian friends Tim and Susan Wallis. Chasing Bonelli's Eagles brought me into contact with Dr Stuart and Jacqui Gregory and their fantastic family. More recently Jonathan Kemp from Limoux has also become a birding companion and Serge Nicolle, an extraordinary artist and naturalist, is sadly my only French birding friend.

The Cathar village of Minerve – just a kilometre or so from our house

Perhaps the most amazing meeting was with Rod Leslie. I had known Rod for a number of years because of his high position in the Forestry Commission and his co-authorship with Mark Avery of the Poyser classic *Birds and Forestry*. Rod is extremely tall and I had no problem spotting him moving through our local market in Olonzac one morning. To this day I am not sure that he appreciated meeting someone from his past living so close to his adopted paradise. More recently I have met Richard and Georgina Pentecost, as well as Craig and Valerie Smith. I have spent a great deal of time in the field with all these people and they have significantly enhanced what for me is one of the greatest pleasures of my life.

The opportunity to regularly visit our French house has gone a long way to filling the void created by retirement.

8.

What of the Future

One of the things that those influential people at The Wildlife Trusts failed to appreciate when I retired from paid work is that once a nature conservationist you are always a nature conservationist. It is not like other jobs where you are glad when it is over and just want a rest. Nature conservation and an obsession with birds is being part of a crusade. It goes on with you until your last breath.

I am just as much a nature conservationist now as when I was being paid. I still remain optimistic, but even so our precious wildlife continues to be threatened and is currently stuck in perpetual decline. How can this be so with so many more people showing an interest and joining the plethora of wildlife and conservation organisations?

To begin with, if you look around the world, the more desecration there has been in a particular country then the higher the membership of its conservation organisations. To put it crudely, people only wake up to the problem when it is already too late. Our elected politicians at every level see protecting our precious wildlife and environment as something that can be added on if we can afford it. They also see people who are lobbying for that protection as being part of a leisure industry which must take its place alongside other interests. What they cannot seem to grasp is that the environment should be sacrosanct and that we, the human race, are only as healthy as that environment because we are part of it. In other words ALL government policies should have protecting the environment and biodiversity as an element of primacy. You can spend all the money you like on health and so on, but if the environment is in a poor state then I would suggest that this money is being wasted.

In my experience many politicians will pay lip service to protecting the environment and even set up schemes to appear to be making good things happen. Take the reaction to the Convention on Biological Diversity (CBD), which the UK Government signed up to in 1992 in Rio de Janeiro. Biodiversity Action Plans were an outcome of this and local authorities quickly moved to set up BAP groups involving all and sundry in their instigation. We now have BAPs everywhere, but have they helped the decline of our wildlife? I believe that the answer is a resounding NO. They are frankly merely talking shops and they take so much time to take any action. I also know of action plans which list certain actions as being potentially damaging and yet these damaging activities continue to be carried out regularly. Nothing is done about stopping these. It is easy to come up with lots of plans but unless ALL actions are activated the whole process is useless. In short they consist of too much process and not enough action.

At least 65 pairs of Little Ringed Plovers nest on shingle banks in the Tywi valley

Where does the fault lie? Firstly the local authorities have very little cash with which to activate the BAPs and secondly the Government Agencies have been stripped of both their power and their dignity and do little to follow up with reinforcement. The police can be helpful with matters of wildlife crime, but habitat damage is probably a bit too specialist for them. However, a partnership between the police and the agencies could work; it certainly worked well in North Wales a year or two ago. A good example of how badly the system works exists in the Tywi Valley near my home in Carmarthenshire. We have a very substantial population of 65 or more pairs of Little Ringed Plovers nesting in this area on natural dynamic shingle banks. It has been noted on the Biodiverstity Action Plan and on the Site of Special Scientific Interest notification that the digging out of the gravel banks is an activity which is damaging for these birds. After supplying photographs of a farmer doing exactly this with a bulldozer in the middle of summer, no action has been taken by the Countryside Council for Wales (CCW).

The break-up of the Government Agencies which originated as The Nature Conservancy Council has been a big contributing factor in the continued demise of British wildlife. This act of vandalism, carried out by Tory minister Nicolas Ridley in 1989, was a reaction to politicians being embarrassed by the NCC's power and scientific prowess and seeing this getting in the way of what they would describe as progress. The late Max Nicholson, who did so much to get the NCC operating to take action for our wildlife and habitats, would I am sure be mortified if he saw the state of things today. Some tried hard to fight the break up and Sir William Wilkinson, the Chairman of the NCC at the time, rendered himself unwell due to his efforts. Today we have devolved agencies which have little power and a largely demotivated staff.

There have been massive declines in our farmland birds such as Corn Bunting

It is also my belief that the NGOs involved in nature conservation must stand back and see why they have failed to arrest our declines in biodiversity. First of all it is my opinion that we have too many NGOs and many of them only concentrate on single groups or even species. At least the massive RSPB is waking up to the fact that its title does not fit the remit it is fulfilling. It is about much more than birds and has been so for decades. The RSPB remains amongst the most powerful and effective of the modern day environmental NGOs, especially with the political classes. The Wildlife Trusts plays an important role locally, but as I have already mentioned there is a lack of consistency in their output across the UK. To me the Wildfowl and Wetlands Trust still cannot decide what it is. Is it a zoo? Is it a research organisation? Is it a nature conservation body? Its three strands are confusing and I believe create a pull on resources which might be better spent going more effectively in a single direction.

The single group/species organisations are an enigma. Some, like Buglife and Plantlife, punch well above their weight, but you could ask why they exist? Do they believe that plants and insects do not receive enough attention from the bigger charities? Others like the Woodland Trust have a most peculiar agenda in urging everybody that planting trees is the answer to everything when it plainly is not. The most pressing question in these times of financial restraint is will they all survive? There is only so much money to go round and this enormous amount of competition could considerably dilute resources. Surely there has to be some consideration of mergers if some of these organizations are to avoid following The Grasslands Trust and cease to exist.

The other concern I have with our NGOs is whether they have become so dependent on finance from government sources at every level, and also from industry, that they have lost the ability to fight the very things which are leading to the decline of our wildlife. It seems to me that many of the big campaigns are not lead by our NGOs. Indeed, The Wildlife Trusts were well to the back of protestations on culling Badgers during the TB battle. It appears to be online organisations which are now picking up the fight on a number of issues, including Badgers and saving our forests. These have tapped into the concept of people power with great success. We must engage more with politicians.

We should not forget that elected politicians at all levels are public servants, and as they are paid out of our taxes they should consider what is being said by us, the public. To get that appreciation we have to engage. We have to tell them what we want. Sadly, few election candidates now knock on our doors so we get less opportunity to tell them directly.

An example of this lack of engagement was borne out in my native Suffolk. Natural England came up with a plan to reintroduce White-tailed Eagles into East Anglia. There was uproar from a few landowners connected to the discredited organisation Songbird Survival. They alleged that livestock would not be safe with these great birds in the sky. Absolute rubbish, but they won the day because those who did want the birds did not come forward and say so. The birding fraternity was deafening in its silence.

What The Wildlife Trusts have been good at is raising the awareness and need for marine conservation. Being an island ensures that we have many marine areas of great importance. Once again Government has been painfully slow to recognise this. Small moves forward are being made and hopefully continued pressure will get the job done.

Fin Whale in the Celtic Deep – it is essential that we conserve our marine environment

I believe that the NGOs need to get together and consider their future. While the RSPB is going through a process of thought this may be THE moment for all wildlife NGOs to join in that process.

One of the biggest threats to our wildlife remain the dinosaurs who refer to themselves as the 'True Countryman'.

This arrogant grouping is usually well to the right in its thinking and wants to maintain the dominance of the human race over all else. Despite all the scientific evidence to the contrary they pursue their beliefs, which are utter nonsense, that predators should be culled or even removed altogether for the sake of smaller species. It is hard to believe that most of these people really care about anything except their beloved gamebirds or racing pigeons. At least a lot are honest enough to say as such, unlike the people behind Songbird Survival, which I believe is a smoke-screen by shooting people and pigeon-fanciers to get protection for raptors rescinded.

These people still carry on as if the law does not affect them. The scandalous situation with the poisoning of birds of prey, and in particular the almost complete extermination of the Hen Harrier as a breeding species in northern England, is a serious crime and it is amazing that few landowners have been prosecuted. It is frankly embarrassing when travelling abroad to concede that the UK is as bad, or if not worse, at destroying wildlife as anywhere else. We are in no position to preach to others.

I realise that all of the thoughts in the paragraphs above are very negative, but I do passionately believe that if we are to improve things then we need to find a fresh starting point. In the last two decades very large sums of money have been spent on nature conservation. From what we can gather from on-going surveys, our wildlife continues to decline despite these efforts. We can point the finger at industrialists and governments, but what could we, the nature conservationists, have done differently? Have we tried to be too broad in our approach? Have we forgotten the real reason we are here?

It is a hard thing for me to say, but I actually believe that a lot of conservationists can pose a big threat to us ever improving the situation. There are too many internal arguments and people fighting their corner for us all to come together for the common good. There is a breed of conservationist who wants every bit of science carried out before taking action. We do not have that much time. As I hinted earlier, many are against radical projects like Oostvaardersplassen in The Netherlands for all sorts of spurious reasons, yet we have nothing comparable in the UK, no single site with such great biodiversity and which attracts over 200,000 visitors each year.

At least The Wildlife Trusts and the RSPB are now working on landscape-sized projects which will take us at least some way towards redressing the balance. We must get behind these organisations and encourage them to do much, much more. There are huge upland areas in the UK which are very unproductive for agriculture. Frankly shooting seems like a totally unsustainable option, especially if the loss of Hen Harriers, Golden Eagles and other raptor species is the price that we have to pay. How much more we would respect politicians if they grasped the mettle and set up a

Government-sponsored Large Area Project somewhere in these regions. If done well this could lead to far more jobs and regional income than any activity that goes on there now.

One thing that seems certain to me is that we have to encourage more young people to take up birding or any other interest in the natural world. I have not forgotten the profound inspiration that I got from those early encounters with adults. My relationship with Mr Benson at school was absolutely paramount in getting me hooked on birds. I know we have RSPB Wildlife Explorers and The Wildlife Trusts' Wildlife Watch groups, but is there more we can do as individuals?

Together with my son Jeremy's family in Canada

My own grandchildren have had an idyllic childhood, being brought up in such exotic places and, thanks to their enlightened parents, always being close to nature. They are growing up fast and Morris, the oldest, is an enthusiastic sportsman. He will try anything, but cross-country skiing is his main passion. He is also a competent musician and his academic achievements are excellent. Tara is more artistic and this comes through in her love of dancing and acting, while she also plays the trombone. She too likes skiing but has worried me a bit lately in taking up wrestling as a sport! Lastly the youngest, Holly, is a bookworm and reads so much. She has a great sense of humour and in her words "loves creepie-crawlies". She too is a keen skier.

All three have a real love of the wilderness and the wildlife that occurs there. This gives me enormous hope that they will keep my love of the natural world alive and hopefully influence their peers as well.

I have come across an initiative which originated in the United States thanks to Englishman Richard Crossley. It is called, appropriately, 'Pledge to Fledge' This is an attempt to persuade birders across the world to engage with people of all ages and get them hooked on birds.

Here is the pledge:

I pledge to actively share my enthusiasm for birds with non-birders by taking them into the field to show them birds

*and foster their own appreciation for birds whenever possible.
I will strive to be friendly, patient, helpful, and welcoming
when approached by non-birders or asked about birds by
acquaintances. I believe that individual birders, as part of
an international grassroots movement, can effect positive and
profound change for our shared birds and their future.*

Go to www.globalbirdinginitiative.org for further
information and click on 'Pledge To Fledge'.

I was lucky enough to receive this sort of help at just the
right age and I have tried to live by this pledge all my life.
People who worked with me in those early days did not even
know they were showing an interest in birds. My wife used
to urge me at dinner parties not to mention birds until at
least the dessert course, to give people a chance to enjoy their
meal. That was a challenge I could not always achieve.

From experience I know that a lot of birders have a long
way to go in terms of sharing their knowledge. I cannot
believe the snobbery that exists with some people about
their interest in birds. Many people are inward-looking and
reluctant to share their love of birding. Worse still, some
with inflated opinions of their own knowledge look down on
anyone who lacks the knowledge and ability to reach their
perceived standard. What is of greatest importance is the
birds. If we take the time to share our passion with others

there will be more people prepared to fight to keep their interest and the birds alive.

Returning to birds and birdwatching, the pastime has developed considerably since I first started going out in my teens. Indeed it is unrecognisable from those pioneering days. My involvement started at a time when most birdwatchers were people of the professional classes. As most of the old literature shows, these people tended to be military officers, men of the church and school teachers. They were the only people with the time and money to buy optics and to go out looking for birds. In the 1950s people did not have casual clothes. You either wore your working clothes or your Sunday best. Hence many birdwatchers at that time set out wearing a tweed suit complete with tie and hat and sometimes, if it was wet, accompanying this by wearing wellington boots. There was no goretex in those days. Most carried 'field glasses' and these generally had low magnification. If they were lucky enough to have a telescope it would be a large brass affair with tubes that you pulled out for magnification. To see anything you would have balance it on a gate post or, worse still, lie on the ground and somehow prop it up on your knees. It is therefore unsurprising that little was ever seen out over the sea in those early days.

This was a period of time which was only just at the end of the great collecting era, when many ornithologists of the day spent their time killing birds to make into zoological specimens. They saw no problem with this, and many of the old books relate that, as they were mostly deeply religious, God would continue to provide more of these wonderful creatures.

In my early days and being from a fairly humble background it was very difficult to meet like-minded souls. I have already told the story of meeting Brian Brown, and this was probably my biggest bit of luck because he, by introducing me to Minsmere, opened up a completely new world.

Digital photography and a stabilised lens have allowed me to take flight shots like this one of a Short-toed Eagle

My how it has changed today. Now there is a huge market in specialist clothing and many people seem to believe that it is now necessary to make a fashion statement when out birding. There is almost a fashion element to binoculars and telescopes, because surely the top of the range items are all as good as each other. Now every birder carries a camera, if not a digital SLR then a small camera which they can attach to their telescope and digiscope the birds in question.

Digital photography alone has revolutionised birding. Nearly every rare bird is now photographed, making it easier for records committees to judge such records. Caution is still needed, though, because we all know that some people have cleverly constructed or manipulated images which turned out to be fraudulent.

There are so many more people birding today. The membership of the RSPB in my early Minsmere days was probably less than 10,000 people; today it is over 1 million. The introduction of computers has seen an increasing number of birding websites and blogs, and this modern technology provides an important source of information for many people. Returning to the Birdfair, the attendances and enthusiasm for this event show just how many people care about birds these days. So there is no longer any need for me to be embarrassed by my interest, and indeed most people meet the news of my obsession with interest and surprising knowledge. I do still get the occasional and boringly familiar comment "Oh Birds – two legged ones?" Have these silly people ever seen any sort of 'bird' with four legs?

Even I now have my own blog. It is a great way of sharing your wildlife experiences and letting off steam when a conservation issue rears its head. You have to keep a sense of proportion and responsibility, but it gives me the chance to say many things without fear of censorship. If you want to check it out go to www.derekbirdbrain.blogspot.com

At least we now have millions of people interested in wildlife to some degree. I am told that at least 12 million British households feed birds. That could encompass the majority of the human population. At least that gives me heart that people will care enough to stand up to decision makers when they want to damage our environment for short term gain.

I am glad that my son Jeremy has decided to stay in Canada and that my grandchildren, Morris, Tara and Holly, will grow up in an amazing environment with so much space and so much wilderness too. They will also enjoy living in a country which seems little affected by the world economic recession and which should give them every opportunity they need.

I am also delighted that my immediate family shares my enthusiasm for the natural world. My son Jeremy has been interested in wildlife for a long time. His chosen profession of geologist shows his thirst for knowledge of how our globe functions. His wife Saskia and the children have spent so much time in wilderness areas around the world and there is no doubting their appreciation of everything they have seen.

The roosting Oriental Pied Hornbills in Jeremy's Brunei garden enthused the whole family

My daughter Bronwen has not always shared my enthusiasm for flora and fauna. She has sprung a few surprises, though, including doing projects at school on agri-environment schemes and bats. She has lifted me considerably in recent years since she has taken up a new career. She is currently working training hotel staff in new software systems – a job which has taken her all around the world. This exposure to fantastic places has meant that she has come face to face with many amazing species. Trying to get me to identify images taken with a mobile phone has led to Bronwen realising the potential of photography, and to her seriously upgrading her equipment and producing wonderful images of everything she sees. There is no doubt that taking my advice and spending a day at the Nairobi National Park really fired up this enthusiasm.

For me, I intend to keep up the crusade whilst I am fit and able. Beryl and I will continue to enjoy our little house in France and keep travelling to see as much of the world as we can. I certainly am keen to continue seeing more bird species and to visit more exciting habitats.

In spite of some of the things I have written, I continue to remain an optimist. Most nature conservationists I have met are optimistic. They have to be, or how could they get up each day and carry on their work? For example, Edgar Milne-Redhead, the great pioneer for the conservation of Black Poplar trees, died at the age of 94 in 1996. At his funeral his son-in-law announced that Edgar was such an optimist that only the previous week he had bought a five-year diary.

You have to believe that ultimately enough people will get the message and join in with the growing band who will fight for our precious wildlife. I hope that this is the case.

If I have inherited the genes of my two grandmothers

then I could have another 20 years left to see more birds and add to my experiences. In order to do that I would need good health, and I hope that this might be the case. I am in no way a religious person, so as far as I am concerned when it is over it is over. In case I am wrong, I wonder if all the bird species in the next life will be lifers?

Acknowledgements

First of all I would like to thank my daughter Bronwen who gave me the idea for this book. She flippantly suggested that she and her brother had merely been minor interruptions in my obsession. I am also grateful to pals Bill Oddie and Chris Packham for their response to a request for two Forewords. I appreciate the extra photographs provided by the photographers listed on page 4.

I am also indebted to Stephen Moss for his encouragement and Simon Papps of New Holland for his patience and enthusiasm during the writing process. Finally I owe everything to all the numerous people who I have bumped into during my life, many who appear in this book. Most especially to all the wonderful people I have met and befriended in the Nature Conservation and Natural History worlds.

Other Natural History Books by New Holland

Advanced Bird ID Handbook: The Western Palearctic
Nils van Duivendijk. Award-winning and innovative field guide covering key features of every important plumage of all 1,350 species and subspecies that have ever occurred in Britain, Europe, North Africa and the Middle East. Published in association with the journal *British Birds*.
£24.99 ISBN 978 1 78009 022 1
Also available: *Advanced Bird ID Guide: The Western Palearctic* (£14.99 ISBN 978 1 84773 607 9).

Atlas of Rare Birds
Dominic Couzens. Amazing tales of 50 of the world's rarest birds, illustrated with a series of colour maps and stunning photographs of little-known species such as White-eyed River Martin and Ivory-billed Woodpecker. Endorsed by BirdLife International.
£24.99 ISBN 978 184773 535 5

Bill Oddie's Birds of Britain and Ireland
Bill Oddie. New edition of a comprehensive field guide to more than 200 species of birds, written in the author's own inimitable style and illustrated with superb colour artworks by top artists.
£12.99 ISBN 978 1 78009 245 4
Also available: *Bill Oddie's Introduction to Birdwatching* (£9.99 ISBN 978 1 78009 410 6).

The Birdman Abroad
Stuart Winter. A gripping account of the overseas escapades of Britain's best-known birding journalist, from showdowns with illegal bird-trappers in Malta to heart-warming tales of conservation in Africa and meetings with big names in birding.
£7.99 ISBN 978 1 84773 692 5

Birds of Africa South of the Sahara
Ian Sinclair and Peter Ryan. Fully updated edition covering more than 2,100 species in full colour over 359 artwork plates. The most comprehensive field guide to the continent's birds.
£29.99 ISBN 978 1 77007 623 5

Birds of Indian Ocean Islands
Ian Sinclair and Olivier Langrand. The first comprehensive field guide to the birds of Madagascar, the Seychelles, Mauritius, Reunion and Rodrigues. Covers 359 species in full colour.
£17.99 ISBN 978 1 86872 956 2

Birds: Magic Moments
Markus Varesvuo. This award-winning title is a collection of breathtaking photographs that records fleeting moments of drama and beauty in the everyday lives of birds, and allows us all to enter into this exciting and vibrant world.
£20 ISBN 978 1 78009 075 7
(Also available: *Fascinating Birds* £20 ISBN 978 1 78009 178 5)

Bird Songs and Calls
Hannu Jannes and Owen Roberts. CD with the songs and calls of 96 common British bird species, accompanied by a book giving written details and colour photos of each one. Ideal for learning bird sounds, or for the dawn chorus season.
£9.99 ISBN 978 1 84773 779 3
(Also available: *Woodland Bird Songs and Calls* £12.99 ISBN 978 1 78009 248 5; *Wetland Bird Songs and Calls* £12.99 ISBN 978 1 78009 249 2)

Chris Packham's Back Garden Nature Reserve
Chris Packham. A complete guide explaining the best ways to attract wildlife into your garden, and how to encourage it to stay there. Packed with practical advice on gardening for wildlife and the identification of birds, animals and plants.
£12.99 ISBN 978 1 84773 698 7

Colouring Birds
Sally MacLarty. Ideal gift to help develop a child's interest in birds. Features 40 species outlines – including such favourites as Robin, Blue Tit, Chaffinch and Green Woodpecker – and a colour section depicting the birds as they appear in life.
£2.99 ISBN 978 184773 526 3
Also available: *Colouring Bugs* (£2.99 ISBN 978 1 84773 525 6).

The Complete Garden Bird Book
Mark Golley and Stephen Moss. New edition of a best-selling book which explains how to attract birds to your garden and then how to identify them. Packed with more than 500 colour artworks of 70 of the most common and widespread garden bird species.
£9.99 ISBN 978 1 84773 980 3

Creative Bird Photography
Bill Coster. Illustrated with the author's inspirational images. An indispensable guide to all aspects of the subject, covering bird portraits, activities such as flight, and taking 'mood' shots.
£14.99 ISBN 978 1 78009 447 2
Also available: *Creative Nature Photography* (£19.99 ISBN 978 1 84773 784 7).

A Field Guide to the Birds of Borneo
Susan Myers. Covers more than 630 species. The only accurate and comprehensive field guide to the varied avifauna of this biodiversity hot-spot, which comprises Brunei, the Malaysian states of Sabah and Sarawak, and the Indonesian states of Kalimantan.
£24.99 ISBN 978 1 84773 381 8

A Field Guide to the Birds of South-East Asia
Craig Robson. New flexi-cover edition of the region's only comprehensive field guide. Fully illustrated in colour. Covers all 1,300 species recorded in Thailand, Vietnam, Singapore, Peninsular Malaysia, Myanmar, Laos and Cambodia.
£24.99 ISBN 978 1 78009 049 8

Also available: *A Field Guide to the Mammals of South-East Asia* (£35, ISBN 978 1 84537 735 9), *A Field Guide to the Reptiles of South-East Asia* (£35 ISBN 978 1 84773 347 4).

The Garden Bird Year
Roy Beddard. Gives both birdwatchers and gardeners insights into how to attract resident and migrant birds to the garden, and how to manage this precious space as a vital resource for wildlife.
£9.99 ISBN 978 184773 503 4

The History of Ornithology
Valerie Chansigaud. The story of more than two millennia of the study of birds. Richly illustrated with numerous artworks, photographs and diagrams, including a detailed timeline of ornithological events.
£17.99 ISBN 978 1 84773 433 4

The Mating Lives of Birds
James Parry. Bird courtship and display is one of the most spectacular events in the natural world. This beautiful book examines everything from territories and song to displays and raising young.
£19.99 ISBN 978 1 84773 937 7

The Naturalized Animals of Britain and Ireland
Christopher Lever. Authoritative and eminently readable account of how alien species were introduced and naturalized, their status and distribution, and their impact. Includes everything from the Ruddy Duck to the Red-necked Wallaby.
£35.00 ISBN 978 1 84773 454 9

New Holland Concise Guides
Ideal first field guides to British wildlife for adults and children. Each covers between 150-300 species in full colour, contains up to 800 colour artworks, comes in protective plastic wallet and includes a fold-out insert comparing species. Series published in association with The Wildlife Trusts.

Titles in the Concise Guide series are as follows (all £4.99):
- *Bird* (ISBN 978 1 84773 601 7)
- *Butterfly & Moth* (ISBN 978 1 84773 602 4)
- *Garden Bird* (ISBN 978 1 84773 978 0)
- *Garden Wildlife* (ISBN 978 1 84773 606 2)
- *Herb* (ISBN 978 1 84773 976 6)
- *Insect* (ISBN 978 1 84773 604 8)
- *Mushroom* (ISBN 978 1 84773 785 4)
- *Pond Wildlife* (ISBN 978 1 84773 977 3)
- *Seashore Wildlife* (ISBN 978 1 84773 786 1)
- *Tree* (ISBN 978 1 84773 605 5)
- *Wild Flower* (ISBN 978 1 84773 603 1)

New Holland European Bird Guide
Peter H Barthel and Paschalis Dougalis. The only truly pocket-sized comprehensive field guide to all the birds of Britain and Europe. Features more than 1,700 beautiful and accurate artworks of over 500 species, plus more than 500 distribution maps.
£10.99 ISBN 978 1 84773 110 4

Newman's Birds of Southern Africa
Kenneth Newman, updated by Vanessa Newman. Revised, updated and expanded edition of the classic field guide. Includes 3,500 colour artworks.
£19.99 ISBN 978 1 77007 876 5

Nick Baker's Bug Book
Nick Baker. A fascinating insight into the world of the mini-beast. Includes tips on how to locate, study, identify them.
£9.99 ISBN 978 1 84773 522 5

Pelagic Birds of the North Atlantic: an ID Guide
Andy Paterson. Innovative new guide, printed on waterproof paper, gives annotated illustrations of every plumage of every pelagic species which could be encountered in the North Atlantic.
£9.99 ISBN 978 1 78009 228 7

Penguins: Close Encounters
David Tipling. The vibrant and exciting world of penguins is shown in all its glory using 140 images by one of the world's top wildlife photographers. Covers all aspects of their life and behaviour and includes all of the world's penguin species.
£20 ISBN 978 1 78009 247 8

Peregrine Falcon
Patrick Stirling-Aird. Beautifully illustrated book detailing the life of this remarkable raptor, including hunting, courtship and raising young. Contains more than 80 stunning colour photographs.
£14.99 ISBN 978 1 84773 769 4
(Also available: *Kingfisher* £12.99 ISBN 978 1 84773 524 9; *Barn Owl* £14.99 ISBN 978 1 84773 768 7)

The Profit of Birding
Bryan Bland. The author is one of birding's greatest story-tellers, and birders and non-birders alike will enjoy the humorous anecdotal narrative, which is accompanied by many of the author's exquisite line-drawings
£14.99 ISBN 978 1 78009 124 2

SASOL Birds of Southern Africa
Ian Sinclair, Phil Hockey and Warwick Tarboton. Fully updated edition of the world's leading guide to southern Africa's 950 bird species. Each is illustrated in full colour and has a distribution map.
£19.99 ISBN 978 1 77007 925 0

The Slater Field Guide to Australian Birds
Peter Slater, Pat Slater and Raoul Slater. Fully updated edition of the classic comprehensive field guide. Features more than 750 species depicted over 150 colour artwork plates. The most portable complete guide to the country's birds available anywhere.
£15.99 ISBN 978 1 87706 963 5

Steve Backshall's Deadly 60
Steve Backshall. Join the author on his most daring adventure yet. Best-selling title which accompanies the popular BBC TV series *Deadly 60*.
£9.99 ISBN 978 1 84773 430 3
(Also available: ***Steve Backshall's Most Poisonous Creatures*** £9.99 ISBN 978 1 78009 462 5)

Tales of a Tabloid Twitcher
Stuart Winter. The key birding events and personalities, scandal and gossip of the past two decades and beyond seen through the eyes of a birding journalist. A 'must-read' book for all birdwatchers.
£7.99 ISBN 978 1 84773 693 2

Top 100 Birding Sites of the World
Dominic Couzens. An inspiration for the traveling birder. Brings together a selection of the best places to go birdwatching on Earth, covering every continent. Includes 350 photos and more than 100 maps.
£19.99 ISBN 978 1 78009 460 1
(Also available: ***Top Birding Sites of Europe*** £22.99 ISBN 978 1 84773 767 0)

The Urban Birder
David Lindo. Even the most unpromising cityscapes can be havens for birds, and The Urban Birder shows you how via a series of remarkable stories, from run-ins with gun-toting youths in London to migration-watching from skyscrapers.
£9.99 ISBN 978 1 78009 494 6

See www.newhollandpublishers.com for further details and special offers